SOUTH NODE ASTROLOGY

UNCOVERING YOUR SOUL'S KARMIC INHERITANCE

ELIZABETH SPRING, M.A.

ARCHEON PRESS

~To You, the Reader~

"Tis the good reader that makes the good book; in every book he finds passages which seem to be confidences or asides hidden from all else and unmistakably meant for that ear; the profit of books is according to the sensibility of the reader; the profoundest thought or passion sleeps as in a mine, until it is discovered by an equal mind and heart."

Ralph Waldo Emerson

CONTENTS

PREFACE

I want to acknowledge my mentor, Steven Forrest, for having inspired me to look to "the chart beneath the chart"—to the potential of Evolutionary Astrology. This type of astrology honors the evolution of the Soul through time and the efforts of each of us to learn and grow more in each lifetime.

I also want to acknowledge the other notable branch of Evolutionary Astrology, begun by Jeffrey Green, which looks to the importance of Pluto as well as to the Nodes in the evolutionary journey of the Soul. I see Pluto as the place of the wound, and the South Node as the past life story.

It has been twelve years since the publication of my

first book: *North Node Astrology; Rediscovering Your Life Direction and Soul Purpose*. In the years since its publication I've continued working as a full-time astrologer and have come to realize the importance of both Nodes—North and South. Originally, I was blinded by the wisdom of the North Node, but now I've come to see that the South Node holds immense gifts as well, teaching us not only what we've suffered from in the past and what we still need to learn, but that it holds karmic wisdom as well. Although we tend to read the South Node negatively, I believe it is only in the understanding of both Nodes that we truly drink from this wellspring of self-knowledge. And so this writing is the necessary book-end to the Nodal Story.

INTRODUCTION

"Uncovering your Soul's Karmic Inheritance" is an ambitious project. One could debate if it is even possible. Obviously, I believe it is possible because over the course of many years studying mainstream astrology I discovered Evolutionary Astrology and the Nodes. Nothing I had learned before had ever been as rich and exciting as what I saw there.

Evolutionary astrology is simply a way, and a technique, of delving into the journey of the Soul through time. It presupposes the idea that the Soul evolves over many lifetimes and that the imprint of the Soul can be read in the North and South Nodes. We can read that imprint clearest by following the trails of clues in the South Node story. From the sign and house position of the South Node we are able to extract insights into ourselves and how we might avoid some of the slippery slopes of life. We can also see how *not* to sabotage our relationships due to past patterns of behavior.

We can use these insights to help our children, understand our parents, and help understand the dynamics of a love relationship. It's one small factor of many, but it may be an important one. I've often noticed, for example, that when I compare two charts and I see that the South Node of one person lines up, or "conjuncts" (is of the same sign and is close in degree) to the other person's Sun, Moon, or Venus that these two people have had a past life connection before and that they intuitively "know" each other. I've seen that so many times in consultations with clients that it always makes me smile.

We can become spiritual detectives of our own lives. However, it is easy to get overwhelmed with this material. If you are relatively new to astrology, or know nothing about it, I suggest you do not try to read this book from beginning to end. *Just look up your South Node sign in the Appendix and read about it.* It holds insights into both the North and

South Nodes in the description and also how to use this information in a practical manner. *Then look up the "House" that your South Node is in and let that marinate for a bit of time in your psyche.*

Then I'd suggest you look up the South Node Story of several people you are close to and see what you can learn. You only need to know their birthday and year; no time or place.

Then, when you're comfortable with that, start piecing the other clues together the way I suggest in this book to fill out the story. If you stop at the sign and house you could rightly say of this book and technique that it's too simple; whereas if you try to do too much too soon it may seem too complicated. This is not a book to "gulp down" in one sitting; rather use it as a reference book as you learn and unravel the *mystery* that is you.

As Albert Einstein once said:

"The most beautiful thing we can experience is the mysterious. It is the source of all true art and science. He to whom this emotion is a stranger, who can no longer pause to wonder and stand rapt in awe, is as good as dead: his eyes are closed."

~Living Philosophies

I hope you enjoy this ancient astrological process of uncovering the story of your Soul through time, knowing that as we work to evolve and advance in each lifetime we grow from learning what didn't work in the previous life. We learn from our mistakes and glimpse as well into the "gold in the shadow" of the South Node. *~ Elizabeth*

YOUR SPIRITUAL DETECTIVE
STORY

The astrology of the Nodes, and the South Node in particular, is a powerful, potent piece of information. I hope in this book to give you a way—a technique—for understanding your Nodes—a way to follow the evolutionary journey of your Soul's life. This is not about discovering the factual history of that life; that you were a peasant in England in 1740. No, this is the emotion-spiritual narrative of what carries over from life to life. The clues to this story are in the North and South Nodes of your chart and they give hints as to how you lived, how you suffered and grew, and what you can do to live your best life now.

. . .

What happened in a previous life carries over into this life and gets repeated until the lesson is learned. When we're born it's actually like waking from a dream; we may not remember the facts of the past life story but we awaken with an "emotional hangover." We don't remember the facts, but the feelings are there, and they often include feelings of confusion, unfinished business and emotional storminess.

This *feeling-story* will repeat itself in this life until we do some spiritual soul searching.

This story of the South Node tells us the past life re-incarnational narrative: particularly what we didn't get right in a previous life, what we suffered from, and sadly, what emotional baggage we're bringing over into this life. It tells us how we're likely to react under stress and what we're bringing forward into new relationships. It sheds light on how we tend to sabotage ourselves, although there is "gold in the shadow of the South Node." Yet still our life purpose is intimately connected to our ability to heal our South Node tendencies.

. . .

We all come into this world with our past life narratives just beyond the scope of memory. We don't have to know astrology to heal and grow into all we can be, but it helps. Like in psychotherapy if you become aware of something you can begin to heal it. The astrological insight or remedy for this lies in the North Node/South Node axis. The North Node points, like a North Star, to what we are called to do; our life direction and soul purpose. The South Node is the reverse, like the tail of the arrow in the astrolabe on the cover of this book. We go towards the North but we need to understand the South. *When we make conscious what is unconscious we begin to heal the woundedness in the South Node, and we automatically engage the North Node.*

And…what makes the South Node story so relevant to this life now is that the past life story tends *to repeat* in this life—until we see that our old default pattern isn't serving us anymore. And so somewhere midstream in our lives we start incorporating more of our North Node energy. And we still will want to take the "gold" in the shadow of the South Node because we've earned some good karma there as well. When you read about your South Node sign you'll see all of it there.

We know that trauma and drama that is not healed tends to repeat itself. Psychology 101. The astrological truth is that we come into this life with a forgotten unhealed past, and it will be relived in this life until we wake up. What can we learn from our chart about this? What do we still have to learn in this life? If there is any place in your chart that speaks to this issue, it's in the Nodes.

Learning to read your Nodes is like viewing your life as a spiritual detective novel. And I hope, in this book, to give you a way to follow the clues to unravel that story. You can also look up the Nodes of anyone you know and ponder not only compatibility of the two of you, but how to make the most of any relationship by seeing it in a clear light.

Now if you're looking for your Nodes you can find

them in the Appendix in this book, or you can see them on your chart. The North Node looks like tiny earphones, and the South Node, looks like a horseshoe. The North and South Nodes are always opposite each other and are exactly 180 degrees apart. In Vedic astrology they are called Rahu and Ketu, but Indian Vedic astrology understands the Nodes very differently than Western astrology. In my opinion, Vedic astrology is fated, predictive and best for the ancients who lived in a society with little free will.

As you may know, the Nodes aren't planets but are mathematical points calculated by the intersecting orbits between the Sun and Moon. They are the two points where the Moon's orbital path crosses the ecliptic, the Sun's apparent orbital path. The South Node is the lower part of the axis which is always exactly opposite the North Node. The Moon's nodes travel in a retrograde fashion and there is only a small bit of difference between the "true" Node and the "mean" Node; I follow the Mean Node as that is the lineage of my teachers.

. . .

Now many readers of this book don't need to learn the fine language astrology; you might just want to get the message of the Nodes. That's fine, and this book is written partially for you. However, if you're an astrologer already and if you're attempting a reading for yourself or someone else, it's best to first do a traditional examination of the chart first, and then to look at the transits and progressions to see what's happening now. Everyone wants to know "what's happening now."

Then look to the Nodal story following the trail of clues that this book is all about—it should be in agreement with the main story *because the whole chart is Karmic, not just the Nodes.* But there are times when the traditional reading doesn't really explain the whole story; this is when you need a Nodal reading.

So the missing link in the story will often be the story of the Nodes: the work from this book, which can be seen as examining "the chart beneath the chart." It reveals the unconscious and past life dynamics that are relevant to this life.

. . .

Although astrology is growing in popularity these days, we need to go deeper than a mainstream understanding of this soul language. Of course I believe we need to look at the powerful trio of Sun, Moon and Rising Sign in the chart. This tells us an enormous amount about ourselves or our client. But there is more. *Have you ever looked at a chart and thought that there was much more to the story than you're seeing?* That something more is the hidden Nodal story: it holds truths that are metaphorical and mysterious.

This is what I believe, and this is why I am sharing with you the trail of breadcrumbs through this great mystery; through this detective story of your life.

Although I was initially drawn to the wise guidance of simply the North Node in the birth chart, I've come to be in awe of the story of the South Node. If we can learn to read the fullness of this story, of this particular piece of our chart, we can intuit the

7

"parable of our past life." It tells us a Truth that is uniquely ours, and ours alone. It tells us a bit of how we suffered before in the life that preceded this one, and how we are now called to learn from that experience.

In Evolutionary Astrology, which is my lineage under Steven Forest, we believe in the evolution of the Soul through time. It presupposes that we grow towards wisdom through lifetimes and that we are drawn towards a birth at a specific time and place so that we will experience what the Soul needs to experience this time around. Our birth chart shows the result of our previous karmic actions and habits, with the South Node showing what afflicted us in the previous life, what we still need to do, and our default patterns of behavior when we're living unskillfully now. The North Node hints of life direction and soul purpose, giving us guidance like a North Star. The Nodes always work as a pair and together they point to the unfolding of what the Soul wants to learn and do in this lifetime. (It's often a stretch to imagine what the Soul must have been thinking between lives to choose a difficult birth—was it ambition to prove it could endure or overcome such obstacles or what?)

So how does it all work? When an astrologer draws up a birth chart based on that very important birth time and place, it will show tendencies, or probabilities, but it doesn't show destiny. We still have free will. Each choice and every attitude in life builds character, and character and fate are delightfully intertwined. Why is it delightful? Because most astrologers believe in the formula of fate plus character equals destiny. Fate can throw us hard times but we create our destiny by building our character in response to what life presents us with. I love the equation: "Fate plus free will=Destiny." Our fate may be to be born an American male from New Jersey raised by a poor single mother, but our free will choices of expression make all the difference in our destiny. The boy may grow up to be a famous musician or a serial killer—*the same chart* could be played out on a higher or lower octave of expression.

. . .

For me, I sense a plan of divine justice here, and a cosmic pattern that affirms a meaningfulness and a divine dance between the macrocosm and the microcosm: between God and man, between the heavens above and the earth below. Astrology accepts the ancient occult saying "as above, so below, as within, so without." The kind of astrology I practice presumes a relationship between the numinous 'mind of God" and the individual psyche within.

Karma suggests habitual patterns and reflects the usual way or style you have of doing things—and it may continue over many lifetimes. (Look at the South Node.) Some of your old habits will serve you well, others seem to be trouble makers. So karmic patterns are reactive knee-jerk responses—they are your default patterns when you're not paying attention. Karma is not all bad, in fact, just like all the planets and signs can be read in a positive and negative manner, your karma contains your gifts as well as your challenges. The karma in the South Node shows the "gold" as well as the shadows of the previous life. In a nutshell, karma is the law of cause and effect, and it repeats and repeats until it's made conscious.

Unfortunately, not all karma is linked in a fair and obvious manner in this one life—the bad guy sometimes seems to win—but only from this viewpoint in the valley below. The mountain-top karmic view sees and responds to the whole story, so the subject does get mysterious. But who doesn't love to attempt to understand a good mystery?

My purpose in writing this book is to give readers a way to look at their chart that is a little deeper than mainstream astrology—a way to look at what has been called: "the chart beneath the chart." I'm going to share with you a technique that you can use to get glimpses into your subconscious and your Soul's intention for this life.

And for those of you who know just a little astrology I'm going to make it simple enough so that you can read about your South Node Sign and house, and with those insights you may discover—

dare I say—probably as much insight as months with a therapist. We will delve! And as you add on each piece of the puzzle the story grows: what planet is the ruler of your South Node? What sign and house is that planet in? What planets are conjunct, square or opposing your South Node? What is your North Node sign and what house is it in? That's the trail of the metaphysical game in a nutshell. It can be as easy or as hard as you make it. It does require *the alchemy of intuition* to string the clues together and to form a cohesive "Aha!" I think we can do it.

It's an unfolding process and after gaining all the clues to this puzzle, it will be your work to put the pieces together. To do the alchemical work of allowing the rational and the intuitive sides of your psyche to cook on the stove of your psyche like a good stew until the aroma arises; until the moment of the "Aha" comes upon you.

Then you'll recognize that you came into this world with "habits" of grit and gold, challenges and gifts. The South Node contains within it a story, a myth, a truthfulness. Can you recognize it? It tells a parable about you, and hopefully those insights will be something unusually useful. Something which will allow you *not to repeat* the mistakes of the past and to have a better life. You may now understand yourself in a way few people do.

As evolutionary astrologers we must read the signs of the South Node negatively, but there are gifts and karmic "gold" in the shadow of the South Node as well. We have earned some talents and wise ways, so that's why I've included after every sign *"Gold in the Shadow of this South Node."* But primarily we're looking to find the unconscious shadow qualities and distortions of the past life so we can learn from this. *It is in the suffering of the heart, the South Node story, where we are called to heal.* It is the most transformative spot in the whole chart.

The North Node we tend to read positively, as it's full of good advice. And remember that the North and South Nodes always work together as a whole, and are contained in each other like a yin/yang symbol. But to miss the hard part of the story and go right to: "Just tell me what to do!" doesn't really get to the core as deeply. My first book was called: "North Node Astrology: Rediscovering Your Life Direction and Soul Purpose." The North Node is like a personal North Star in pointing to the Soul's ideal direction in this life, whereas the South Node points to what you still have yet to learn. What your work in this life is about. And so we move towards healing the past and going towards the future altogether, with no blinders on. We don't want our 'shadows' dragging along behind us getting us in trouble.

The South Node is also an indicator of how you're likely to love and not love in this lifetime. In it we can see where our blind spots are—those traits that could *sabotage our ability to be in a good relationship*. But we also have our "saving graces" here as well because we earned good karma in the last life too, but the rule in evolutionary astrology is that we read the South Node in its lower octave. That's where it tells the most, and we can then live out the higher octave, the best possibilities.

It's also true that the whole chart is karmic. For

14

example, the planet Pluto shows us something of our wounds in this life, but the South Node points to something deeper and more ingrained. The planet Pluto points to an unconscious soul wound but knowing about our Pluto doesn't give us the potential for change that the South Node does; perhaps because it's a wound that remains more constant rather than a *narrative that can be learned from*. It doesn't have the same potential for life transformation.

Relationships are probably the hardest work we have in this lifetime. Knowing our birth chart helps us become conscious of who we are and what we need to do to live our most authentic lives. Knowing another person's birth chart is...well, it's a *huge* help in understanding them. But most people can't "read" the chart well enough to get the answers they're looking for—and this is where the *South Node* comes in—because if you add that filter to your astrological vocabulary then you've got another potent key to understanding any relationship. And sometimes it brings compassion as well; when we get a glimpse of what the Soul has endured and how it's growing we see the potential for change and growth.

Now when you take your South Node sign and compare it to another person's South Node sign you might end up seeing how a certain chemistry or alchemy could happen. For example, if your Nodes (particularly the *North Node*) is calling for a life of serenity and the comfort and challenges of creating a home, and "his chart" is calling for a life of long adventures and sitting on mountaintops it's going to be hard to make this relationship work.

Or if you're a person who's suffered in a past life from loss of Self by duties and obligations that made you into a "Mrs David Jones," with 6 children as well, you might just find yourself born into this life with a *South Node* in the 7th house of marriage and you intuitively already know that you're not going to want to repeat that past life story again! (You don't even need your astrology chart to point that out. But it's there tucked away discreetly in the South Node if you care to look.)

. . .

Throughout the history of astrology these ancient points have been the keys to understanding the trajectory of the Soul. Like a compass that points North we get good cosmic advice in the North Node and we get the story of the past life journey in the South Node.

The qualities in the North Node are where your Soul longs to go towards in this life, whereas the past life South Node story is not what you want to repeat or to bring forth into a relationship. Although it's not easy to change the ways of the past and unconscious patterns and old hurts, we can become aware of the tenderness in these places in ourselves and choose not to repeat old default patterns of behavior that have gotten us into trouble before. As I touched on before, you can act out all the signs and planets and nodes on a higher octave or a lower octave; it's up to you.

It isn't surprising really that in the beginning of our lives we live out our South Node 'repetitions of the scenarios' from the past life and those patterns can *save or sabotage* our current relationships. It's the most sensitive piece of information or insight we can know about ourselves and another person, whether we may be dating them or in relationship with them; whether it be your mother, father, child or lover.

Now I know the word "sabotage" is a jolting word to use, and that love itself doesn't sabotage, but the distortions and emotional poverty from lack of love in the past does sabotage the psyche. For example, when we don't get good-enough parenting when young, we start off life with a deficit, but it's not unrepairable. The South Node holds that emotional memory of love or lack of love from your last life as well as this one.

Every romantic movie and love song reminds us of how love *saves* us. but it's in the therapist's office that one hears the story of how love *sabotages* us. It's all so unconscious: again, it's as if we woke up into this life with an emotional hangover not remembering what happened during the night's dream. We don't get an instruction manual at birth, so we only act from what we know and feel.

So the South Node shows how you will tend to act in a relationship when you are stressed and acting out your worst default behaviors, as well as how you have 'saving graces' which you can also use to nurture and heal a relationship. What insight this can bring when you are first meeting someone or when you're looking for ways to save a relationship! Insights into blind or unconscious default patterns are priceless. They can help us change, but they should never be used to shame or blame; how you use this information is an ethical issue.

So we know that there's a tendency to repeat our South Node story in the beginning of this life. If in the life that preceded this one we survived by fast talking and quick knowledge (perhaps Gemini South Node) we will tend to repeat the same survival scenario because it's ingrained in our psyche like genetic material is ingrained in DNA. The whole new science of epigenetics is exploring this now: how we carry our family and cultural inheritance in our DNA or psyche somewhere.

. . .

When do we change South Node patterns? Some people will never lose the imprint of their past and they'll carry it into all they do. Others will become conscious of their own ways through self-reflection, therapy, or astrological insight but no one knows when we are "released" from the most painful habits of our past. Perhaps never entirely, but God or the Universe certainly seems to want to help us do this at the major turning points of the first and second Saturn Returns—at ages 29 and 59, and at the Uranus Opposition around age 42. *And* the Nodal Returns happen throughout our life approximately every 18.5 years. So at every return of the Nodes to their birth position, at roughly ages 18, 37, 55,74 and 83 the karmic wave breaks again and we can delve deeper and higher into our Life Journey. We will always benefit from knowing the past life story but at those ages we become particularly open to bringing into consciousness that which was unconscious. And we often have a special energy at those times to make a change.

I hope this book will guide you to do some personal *Soul Retrieval* so that you will feel a sense of integrity and not bitterness in your life. And I hope it helps you with the sweetest and hardest 'yoga of relationships' in the best possible way; through deep understanding and compassion. What a gift we've been given with these ancient *footprints of the gods* on our charts!

DIVING INTO THE DEEP: THE TECHNIQUE

*T*he Questions To Hold In Mind:

- What were you trying to do in your last life? And earlier in this one? How did you survive? (South Node)
- What did you suffer from then? (South Node)
- What didn't you know how to do in the past that could have helped you then, and now? What do you still need to learn? (South Node)
- Now what can you do to transform your life? (North and South Node)
- Now what can you do to transform your relationships based on what you know

about yourself and another person? (North
and South Nodes)

One of the things that will be important to
remember in this process of discovery is not *to
shame oneself—or another*—for what we may see
as flaws. We all have them and although you may
be nodding your head in agreement at that cliché it
is crucial to remembering it as we do this work. All
of us are born into this incarnation with unfinished
business and less than a perfect record from a
previous life. That's why we've reincarnated again;
to try again, and to heal.

So please don't take what you learn here and say
"Well he had a South Node in Aquarius squared by
Mars and he was a cold angry person who simply
doesn't know how to do relationships." Yes, there
may be some truth to that as a reflection of what he
didn't get right in the past, but we must allow each
other the chance to use our free will to change. In
this case, he would have a North Node in the warm
and heart-felt sign of Leo, and he would have all the
potential for being a warm and caring person. And
that Mars may have been square the Nodes, but was
it anger he had to change or was that Mars in Taurus

reflecting he came here in part to learn how to trust again? If you are a trustworthy person you may be just the right person to show him how to open his heart again. So be careful with judgements...

Let's start at the beginning, as we begin with The Technique of reading the nodal story. I suggest you take out pen and paper and maybe even a little notebook as you work through all the clues to your story.

The Core Vocabulary

*What is the sign of your South Node? (It's based on your birth day and year, and will be above the description of the sign at the beginning of each chapter.)

*What house is the South Node in? (You'll need to have a copy of your birth chart for this one. Idea: get a free birth chart online, like on Astro.com)

*What is the Ruling Planet of your South Node? And what House is it in? Each sign has a Ruling Planet which will be explained in its chapter. You'll see I've chosen to use the contemporary rulers of each sign, rather than traditional. Simply a choice, and the lineage I follow.

*What are the aspects to your South Node? We'll be discussing planets conjunct each other (around 0- 8 degrees from each other), squaring (90 degrees) and opposing (180 degrees) the South Node. The trines (120 degrees) are nice, but sorry--they may be supportive or simply "tea and sympathy" but not relevant for this soul work.

*What sign is Your North Node? (It's always exactly opposite your South Node by 180 degrees, and will be integrated into the description of your South Node.)

*What house is your North Node in? Again it will be the house exactly opposite where your South Node is. You will see the glyph that looks like a set of earphones—that's it!

* Also keep in the back of your mind your Sun and Moon sign. Why did my Soul choose to be born with this Sun and Moon sign? How is it useful to me in getting to the soul direction of the North Node? The qualities of these luminaries and your Nodes are the keys to this puzzle. And because

Sun/Moon sign astrological information is so common in books and on the internet ,I'll not be delving into that here. I want to share with you instead *the piece of the puzzle that you may not know, and the technique of following the trail of clues to your past life story—and Soul Purpose through the Nodes* –this gives you something quite interesting to ponder. It gives you the trail of clues in helping you unpack the parable of your past life story and what *you are called to do here now*.

So this is a very specific technique—a puzzle really —that will give you insights as you do it. And I will be providing extra information when it looks confusing, but these are the basic clues that we'll use to put together in our alchemical vessel or cooking pot, and you'll need to let it cook there in your psyche, until you get what the psychiatrist Carl Jung called the *Numinous Third* or *the "Aha" moment* which arises when the cooking ingredients start sending out their aromas. This is the work of a lifetime, and it will be something you can return to again and again.

SOUTH NODE ARIES (NORTH NODE LIBRA)

*T*his is your South Node if you were born between these dates:

Sept 13 1939-May 24 1941

June 17 1958-Dec 15 1959

Jan 8 1977-July 5 1978

Aug 1 1995-Jan 25 1997

(For more recent dates, google your South Node sign for your birthday and year)

.   .   .

The Ruling Planet for this South Node in Aries is Mars, and Venus is the ruling planet for its North Node Libra. We can tell a lot about this Nodal story right from the planets themselves.

In the past, Aries South Node people have been *spiritual warriors*: you fought for the good and defended the innocent. This doesn't mean you were necessarily a soldier, but you had to summon all your *courage* (a key word for Aries) to survive and live a life with integrity. You liked to be the hero/heroine in your own stories, and you had the drive and initiative to be a pioneer; to roll up your sleeves and get to work. Patience is not a virtue for you, you'd call that procrastination. Aries are independent types and fear loss of control and becoming dependent on others.

The *past pattern* of self-centeredness and willfulness has been necessary for survival. The challenge in the past was that you saw injustice, cruelty and misuse of power and you didn't just stand by and watch. Yet *your needs* could have been lost under the demands of others unless you spoke up, and now your Soul has to learn about the balance between dependence and independence. Seems easy to understand but relating fairly and harmoniously in this life isn't an easy thing to do when you were dismissed and overlooked in the past…and maybe killed for your beliefs as well.

In fact, chances are you weren't just treated unfairly, chances are you had to fight for your life and principles in some way—adrenaline was rushing through your veins as you were caught up in a battle; literal or otherwise. Anger and fear, as well as the dramatic and intensely exhausting drama of this South Node in Aries gave you the reflexes of a warrior in this life.

And remember that this is what you came into this life with as a baby; this feeling that you must fight for your rights and beliefs, that you must be heard, and that people aren't necessarily looking out for your best interests. In this new life you're born into, your family of origin may be the subtle or not so subtle new battleground for you to play this out on.

You may have to do this for a while, but the Soul Intention is to let the defensiveness go.

Now it's going to be important for you to find ways to calm down, release tension and allow all forms of beauty and harmony to heal you—sounds like a call for Venus, doesn't it? You are indeed called to find the serenity of Venus in this life, as Venus rules your North Node Libra and is the prescription for an overactive Mars. Don't be hard on yourself; your Soul has known the horror of trauma and drama and has chosen this life to heal from that. You can dare to slow down now and weigh and balance all the different ways you think about things.

Ways you may sabotage yourself and your relationships unconsciously:

How does this relate to Love? Aries South Nodes know the world of passion, but love itself is bigger than passion, and sometimes less exciting. Love sabotages us when we act out of a passion that is overly dramatic and that has you as the only hero/heroine on stage. Love saves and heals when you call on the wisdom of your Aries courageousness and do what must be done without the competitive or adrenaline-laced attitude of an unhealed Aries attitude. Aries may be fueled by necessity, but the Aries South Node vision can be larger than the "every man for himself" attitude that is the low road for Arians.

The "emotional memory of love" for Aries South Node has a tinge of solitariness to it. Can you trust? Who will help you survive? In a past life, your Soul may have died alone—the family wasn't gathered around the bedside, but you may have died on the battlefield or in the hospital bed waiting for the nurse that didn't arrive in time. You know instinctively that you had to be quick and self-watchful to survive in the past—but now, with this in your past, you are still called to develop trust in others as well as trust in yourself. If you can pause in your reactivity long enough in this life (slow down that response to "fight of flight"!) you may find that loneliness turns into soul-nourishing solitude, and instead of dying, you find that the numinous "Other" was there all along.

. . .

There may still be in you now an addiction to intensity, passion, ambition or anger that is used as personal fuel. You may feel that you still have to fight for yourself and what you believe in because you're still not heard and your causes and beliefs must be fought for. Try to give up the battle; the war is over.

This South Node can be quite hard on relationships as you may come across as leading with your Ego and not your true Self, and you may be unable to forgive or to see all sides of a question. It may take a long time to truly trust. When your existence was a matter of life or death, as it was in a previous life, then you had to be not only assertive but aggressive at times. Now you are called to relationships, not rugged individualism. Your Soul benefits from the "yoga of relationships" and it's not going to come easy, yet it's where you will learn to find the sweet spot of balance and peace.

Whenever possible let go of the need to be "right"

or to do things perfectly. The idea now is to find the sacred in the ordinary things of life as they come to you naturally and without effort. Humorously one might say that the antidote for you is to show up at your friend or partner's house with flowers and wine in hand and invite them to a picnic on the beach. And if they say no, you go anyway, with your camera and notebook in hand and call it an "artist's date." Look for the beauty to photograph and the insightful words to write. You are meant to be an artist of the Soul in this life.

Now continuing with the Nodal story, look to see where Mars is in your chart as this will tell you something about where some of this behavior is acting out. Look to the house Mars is in. There's a description of each house in the chapter after the signs and you can look to that house as another clue in this evolving story of your past life. We will also look at planets that conjunct, square or oppose the South Node to refine the story more, but this South Node sign in Aries tells us a lot already.

The Gold in the shadow of this South Node:

courage, willingness to begin again, keen intelligence, a purity of heart like the Fool in the Tarot Cards.

Physical problems relating to Aries South Node: headaches, illness or wounds to the head

SOUTH NODE TAURUS (NORTH NODE SCORPIO)

*T*his is your South Node if you were born between these dates:

Mar 4 1938-Sept 12 1939

Oct 5 1956-June 16 1958

July 11 1975-Jan 7 1977

Feb 2 1994-Jul 31 1995

(For more recent dates, google your South Node sign for your birthday and year)

· · ·

There's something innately good about Taurus with its natural affinity for the simple life, the good life, the "close to the earth and home and hearth life." However as a South Node pattern we need to look at what Taurus suffered from in a past life, what you didn't learn and what is called for now.

Life is complex and we are all full of paradoxes. Taurus South Nodes would prefer it to be otherwise; you would like it if 'you would get what you see.' You would like it if what you do reflects your values. What's wrong with that? The Taurus South Node may have enjoyed a life where there were issues around emotional and financial security and you sought to keep things safe and secure—but--! But because "safe and secure" doesn't reflect the full story of Reality you missed out on some Truth and Consequences---and the nuances of life. You may have been naïve and extremely stubborn as you sought to keep things safe, secure and close to home.

Risk-taking would have been avoided, because stability and predictability were the gods of home.

But this attachment to keeping the status quo caused suffering because of its stiffness and conservative narrow mindedness. People and life aren't simple, but if you have this South Node you didn't want to know about that. Change has unnerved you. It caused you to act stubborn and resistant, turning family members and lovers against you. You refused to see the fine print and the complexities. You refused to grow. You tended the garden and put dinner on the table, but when your daughter wanted to marry outside your caste or race or religion you would have turned a blind eye to her suffering. You knew best.

The past patterns, and current default pattern of this South Node asks you to relax your concerns around money, security and possessions as well as being willing to risk losing your current level of comfort to gain a higher state of power and vitality. And peace.

This Nodal pattern with the North Node in Scorpio asks you to not only see the paradoxes of life and to be flexible, but to actually seek out the shadows so as to know the whole story. You are meant to feel your daughter's pain and to risk trying things that innately you consider risky. This Scorpio North Node dares you to explore the dark, the taboo, the unspoken and then to take this ability to see the dark and transform it.

Ways You May Sabotage Yourself and Your Relationships

Venus is exalted in Taurus, meaning that the planetary archetype of Venus naturally and comfortably expresses itself through a grounded, pragmatic and sensual understanding of life.

That is unless you've taken it too far. And this may be the case if your South Node is in Taurus. The South Node always represents the area that we didn't get quite right in a former life, or earlier in this one, so we are called now to release the down side of these habits and traits. Too much emphasis on Venusian security, sensuality and relationships can hint of a touch of laziness or materiality that doesn't leave room for the depth, painful truth, or edginess that Soul Work sometimes requires.

Have you been living in a world of denial or attempting a false security that isn't rooted in deep truth? The South Node in Taurus speaks to the need to move away from the over-dependence on personal resources ("He who dies with the most money wins") or continual security seeking ("This is my house and I don't ever want to consider moving for any reason.")

Too great a concern for the sensual desires of Venus tends towards materialism and the antidote is to move towards your Scorpio North Node. This is about a willingness to risk one's present level of security for a deeper, truer level of security and integrity. This is where the balance is brought in by the Scorpio North Node, which continually wants to know "what's the emotional bottom line truth here? And what do I need to do about it?"

Staying stubborn in your ideas and ideals about how

things should look and be creates trouble. You have tried to simplify things to make it safe and predictable but in doing so you didn't truly do the "work" of relationship. It's been said that to have a good friend (or partner) you have to be a good forgiver. And for you, that means seeing the whole picture: the good, the bad and the ugly…and still finding room for love.

You also may have suffered greatly with issues around money and possessions---by holding on and hoarding. Perhaps hoarding is too strong a word here, but let's imagine that you were poor and hunger was an issue. You might have eaten as much as you could and had a hidden spot for reserves. So you come into this life with a great hunger—and maybe now you grow fat! Who would blame you if they knew the poverty you suffered from in a previous life? And if you felt judged by others because of your possessions and status—or lack of it—you probably judged them as well. So a vicious cycle may have started then and in this life you are meant to re-examine your true values and let go of tendencies to judge others. You are called now to own up to where your fear causes you to do things that aren't part of your values. You may have suffered from the "ends justify the means" and so in this life you need to become willing to look at what the "means" will actually do. It may cause misery.

Also read about your Sun sign's *lower octave of expression* because the qualities of your Sun sign and your Nodal signs are the largest keys to this puzzle. Again because Sun sign information is so common in books and on the internet I'll not be delving into that here. I want to share with you instead the piece of the puzzle that you may not know.

The Ruling Planet for this South Node in Taurus is Venus, and Pluto is the ruling planet for its North Node Scorpio. Venus can be a soothing balm to trauma and drama yet as ruler of the South Node something Venusian may have caused problems in your life. Relationships may have afflicted you, and with Pluto as ruler of North Node you are called to go deeper into the complexities of relationships. Go beyond the obvious. Look deeper.

. . .

We can tell more about this Nodal story right from the planets themselves. You will want to look up to see where Venus is located in your chart—what sign and house is it in, and is it making aspects? Look to the next chapters and see if you can add more nuances to the Venusian story.

Gold in the Shadow of this South Node: a loyalty, a sweet and enduring sensuality, a noble sense of responsibility and caring.

Physical Problems Related to South Node Taurus: illness or injury to the neck and to the sense organs: eyes, ears, nose, mouth

GEMINI SOUTH NODE
(SAGITTARIUS NORTH NODE)

*I*f your birthday falls between these dates, your South Node is in Gemini:

Sept 15 1936-March 3 1938

April 3 1955-Oct 4 1956

Oct 28 1973-July 10 1975

Aug 2 1992-Feb 1 1994

(For more recent dates, google your South Node sign for your birthday and year)

. . .

With a Gemini South Node your ruling planet is Mercury and you were born with street smarts. You were savvy! You had a quick witted and sure-footed confidence that was yours and you could handle yourself in any situation. But looking at the South Node negatively which is what we do, you could talk yourself into and out of any situation being a bit of a chameleon. Your knowledge came from hands on experience in the market-place of life, and what you didn't learn from the streets you learned from your elders and siblings. You could have been a pick pocket in London or a verbose charismatic scholar at a University. (Look to your house placement to get hints at what area of life you were playing this out.)

Communication was your strength, and you gathered experiences like a dog gathers fleas. No, I don't mean to say that what you learned was an annoyance or false but rather that the quick fast talking persona couldn't put it all together into wisdom or a life strategy. It was survival by knowledge rather than wisdom.

· · ·

Your North Node is in Jupiter-ruled Sagittarius. Jupiter relates not only to expansion but to Faith. Now it is as if your Soul yearns to look beyond the relativity of everything to find some essential Truth of your own to live by. You need a mountain-top experience where you see the full gestalt of the puzzle of your life. You are leaving behind the impatient, overly logical part of yourself that constantly hungers for more factual information and moving towards gaining a more soul-full resonance that senses a deeper purpose in life.

Your ability to communicate with anybody, and to quickly recognize opportunities and to create bridges between people was a gift. You could have been a writer, a professor or a con artist. Whatever you did though, it would have benefited by more in-depth study or travel that could have deepened and slowed you down. You were stressed and likely over-extended. People liked you; but did they know who you really were, or were they just seeing a facet of a multi-facetted personality?

. . .

This past pattern of survival by quick reflexes and information gathering is now ready to be honed into a more thoughtful philosophic and generous soulfulness. You were born with a youthful addiction to "stay forever young." Why not? It was exciting and fun. But…you suffered from it. You finally got caught in your over-confidence, over-doing and "tripping the light fantastic." You are now ready to do the one thing you were most afraid of before: to commit to one thing or to one person.

Ways You May Sabotage Yourself or Your Relationships Unconsciously

A Gemini wants a best friend in their lover. You want to talk, and in fact, you can be almost warrior-like in love arguments. Verbal sparring keeps you from being bored and spices things up—but you can take it too far. Not everyone loves a friendly verbal debate. Some people call that an argument when you just thought you had a discussion with your best friend. You don't like enmeshment or being smothered by a friend or lover; in fact you're wanting excitement in a relationship. The Gemini

South Node person loves the stimulation of new ideas and things to do; you react to boredom like an allergy.

You may also be afraid to commit. With your options always open you didn't have to take the real risk of saying "This is who I am and this is what I believe." It was your past survival strategy to move around quickly, playing at life, gathering experiences and probably lovers. But what does that add up to on one's deathbed? Very often, unhappiness. A life where you skimmed your way through...

Now, I don't mean to make you sound as if you didn't have reason to do this, I'm sure you did. If you were born the youngest of ten children you might have seen the pressures of the eldest son. Perhaps you saw his unhappiness with too much responsibility and duties put upon him. It could have crushed him. Instead you may have realized that moving away from home kept those dramas away and in taking your freedom you became a traveling musician or snake oil salesman. People probably said of you that you were "a free spirit and forever young." They never heard you speak of your loneliness.

In this life, you would be wise to see your life as a grand quest (Sagittarius trait) where you commit to achievable goals—finish that book you've started and raise your child the best way you know how. This way you'll create "a Life" where your commitments and responsibilities give you the freedom to know not just fleeting happiness, but true joy and contentment. It's all do-able this time around. Your ruling planet Jupiter all brings in an element of luck into your unfolding quest.

Look to see what sign Mercury is in and where Mercury is located in your chart, because by knowing the sign and house of your Mercury you'll be able to intuit more of what part of your life is being activated by this South Node. Another clue in the story.

Gold in the Shadow of the South Node: a magnetic

charisma, intelligence and open-mindedness, a bridge-builder and story-teller, and a good friend in times of need.

Physical problems related to South Node Gemini:

Problems related to the lungs, voice, and hands.

SOUTH NODE CANCER (NORTH NODE CAPRICORN)

*I*f you born between these dates, then your South Node is in Cancer:

March 9 1935—Sept 14 1936

Oct 10 1953—Apr 2 1955

Apr 28 1972—Oct 27 1973

Nov 19,1990—Aug 1 1992

You can find South Node dates after this time on the internet by using the birthday and year.

. . .

Cancer, ruled by the Moon, scores high in instinct and intuition. One of their strongest instinct is the identification with home, hearth, and heart. Cancer is changeable like the Moon, and moody; they can be introverts in the morning cleaning their closets, and extroverts by evening, dancing on the beach by the light of the Moon.

To have Cancer as your South Node hints that you were strongly identified with your family and clan in a former life. You drew your sense of Self from them and you may have been most happy when you were able to nurture, defend and protect them. Sounds good, doesn't it?

But because we read the South Node in its lower expression we see a Soul that was swallowed up in dependency/independency issues within the family. You needed to be needed, and boundaries were blurry. By attending to other's needs you were able to avoid *the existential angst of the hero's journey* where the hero/heroine would go out into the world and slay dragons and find the golden fleece. (Leave that to Aries!) Cancer South Nodes were more likely to stay at home and keep the fires burning there: you would care for the young and the needy ones as they came home from battle.

Although a great comforter of others, you too could get moody, "looney" and flip sides (you are ruled by the Moon which changes shape constantly.) You may have lost yourself in the process of being a caregiver. There's also a chance that you were the youngest child yourself, and as the youngest of the family you may have suffered from all that that entailed—primarily the lack of personal responsibility to mature into all you could be. You might have felt "less than."

Your home was the gilded cage that became your Soul cage. In this life now you are called to leave "home" and to value freedom and honest self-expression—including owning your own strength. You are called out into the world to be independent, and not seduced by applause and other peoples' opinions of you, and to truly set a goal and follow it. (That's the Saturn way in your Capricorn North Node.) You've cried enough tears for yourself and others in a former life and now you need to cultivate a stiff upper lip! Do the work of growing into all you can be, and don't dwell on the process and every mood that comes and goes. Think of them as clouds passing over the mountain; you want to keep your eye on the mountaintop. You are meant to get to the top of that mountain and claim success for yourself in this life.

Ways You May Sabotage Yourself or Your Relationships Unconsciously

Serious, sentimental and sensitive are words that might describe you when you're in love. You can get your feelings hurt quickly by people who don't understand your true nature. You've probably had lifetimes of being protectors of your family and loved ones so it's hard for you to understand uncommitted love and senseless flirting. You need to talk to potential lovers and close friends rather than assume they know your feelings. Not everyone has antennae as sensitive and keen as you do. You can be loyal and willing to work things out when the going gets tough, once you've gotten to a place of trust. Being a bit slow and cautious in relationships is not a bad idea for you.

Now for some people, remembering their night dreams and talking over the possibilities of meaning in a nightmare is perfect therapy. You might cry a few tears. Take a long hot bath, and maybe take a mental health day off from work. But don't do that for too long! This is how you might sabotage yourself with focusing on the *emotional process* of your life so much that you miss the fact that you might have had an important date with someone that day that would have furthered your career or a new relationship. Your career is not just about making money—it's about making a sense of Self. You sabotage yourself when you don't try hard enough to achieve your goals and when you don't make that extra effort to go another mile up towards the mountaintop.

In relationships one can see how you might suffer without having good boundaries—sometimes even a state line between yourself and your relatives. You also suffer when you listen too long and hard to other people's troubles without truly sharing your own stories. Oprah Winfrey has this Nodal combination and she has been wise to take her focus off of her family of origin and replace it with the larger "family" of the world.

Yet as I've written before in my book "North Node Astrology" there is always gold in the shadow of the South Node. And with Cancer there is a warm and tender heart and a willingness to care deeply. This serves South Node Cancer well when it's balanced with the vision and work ethic of the Capricorn Node. When approaching life this way, it's not only savvy, but you're becoming your own authority and author of your own life. So for you, setting high goals and enjoying the view from the top of the mountain will be a peak experience. And that sounds good!

Look to see what sign the Moon is in and where the Moon is located in your chart, so that you'll know what part of your life is being activated by this South Node. Read about it in the chapter on the houses and you'll have another clue to your past life story.

Gold in the Shadow of this South Node: warm tender heartedness, helpfulness, intuitive and psychic nature, a deep knowingness and often a joy to be around.

Physical problems related to South Node Cancer: the stomach, the breast, the emotions.

SOUTH NODE LEO (NORTH NODE AQUARIUS)

*I*f you born between these dates, then your South Node is in Leo:

June 25 1933—March 8 1935

Mar 29 1952---Oct 9 1953

Nov 3 1970—Apr 27 1972

May 23 1989—Nov 8 1990

Dec 19 2007—Aug 22 2009

In a past life you may have lived a life that had little connection to your true Self. Although you were probably well-liked and applauded for your personality, something deep inside you wasn't expressed. You were seduced by both the adulation and expectations of others, and with the Leo tendency towards royalty, you were likely in a position of privilege and status. You had a charismatic "shine" about you that likely drew you into a dramatic or expressive art. But you feared disapproval and rejection. Your big and generous heart probably got bruised and wounded many times.

What you needed then, and what you need now, is the sense of objectivity and individuality that is part of the calling of your North Star--your North Node in Aquarius. You saw the world very subjectively in the past and took everything personally. Part of this was also a tendency to add more drama and pathos to any situation and to feel responsible for everything. With a strong desire to give and receive love, you came across as being controlling, and you felt the tension of that responsibility. Others projected strong feelings of like or dislike onto you and you didn't understand.

. . .

Like the Lion in the Wizard of Oz you needed courage...the French word for courage, Coeur, literally means heart; and although you acted from your heart, chances are you had to reach into your Soul and continually search for it. Sometimes you had it, sometimes you didn't. You could have died from a broken heart and no one may have even known it.

When you have the riches of money and the praise of others it was hard for you to own up to the fact that you were often lonely and feeling trapped by your own drama. In today's world we'd say you "branded yourself" so well in the world, and succeeded so well, that you trapped yourself. There was no freedom. There was limited Soul expression. In your suffering you may have even descended into narcissistic self-pity.

Your old pattern of being seduced by other people's projections and expectations on you of who you are and what you're all about, can be released in this life. You are now called to be free! You are called to authentic Soul expression—to be a rebel, an individualist, and a seeker for Truth. Your North Node in Aquarius wants you to care for the needs of the whole, and like a visionary, to point to what the "whole" (humanity) may need. You may do well this time around as a rebel, free thinker, reformer and visionary. You can see what many of us can't see.

Ways You May Sabotage Yourself And Your Relationships Unconsciously

A Leo South Node in love or as a good friend, is loyal, generous and possessive…and sometimes like a cat. You like to be admired and stroked a bit and then let go of. You need a little space to walk around and survey the situation before you "leap" because you can get burned, or burn others with your passionate nature. With your charm and charisma you can learn how to turn the fire on and off as you choose. But be aware that your fiery nature is unique, exciting and not to be treated lightly. You need respect.

. . .

With your South Node in Leo, the archetype of the King or Queen is activated and you may still have a whiff of "entitlement" about you and that doesn't set well with the rest of us mortals. You may not be able to see that about yourself because it was simply a way of being that you became very accustom to in your last life. And now....well, for example, doesn't everyone expect good service at a pricey restaurant? Of course, they do, but after waiting too long for your food, you might be the one who simply stands up, looks around, and with your head held high, walks out of the restaurant. The flair with which you call the valet for your car may impress some, but the waiter who is left to explain it all to the manager is anything but impressed. And your date may have decided that was the last straw. Entitlement isn't flattering on anybody. You suffered.

In this life, especially after your first Saturn Return at age 29, or after any major life learning experience, you may find yourself moving towards your Aquarian North Node. You may feel an astute awareness of the importance of equality and fairness. You could become so objective that others now think you are all in your head and not in your heart. Deep in your Soul you know a balance is needed but it can be confusing for you.

But before you come to this balance you may still have melodramatic tendencies to insist on doing things your own way and taking dramatic risks. When you ask the Universe or God for what you really want and trust that what is right for you will be given, then you're on the right path.

The Sun is the ruler of Leo so look to what sign the Sun is in, and where it's located; what house. The sign and house position will fill in clues as to what area of life your South Node tendencies have played out...can you begin to put a few parts of the story together? Like a good puzzle it requires an intuitive synthesizing to put the pieces together.

Gold in the Shadow of this South Node: generosity of heart, a flair for living, a largeness of spirit, a deep caring and defensiveness for those you love.

. . .

Physical issues with South Node in Leo can be related to the heart and the spine.

SOUTH NODE VIRGO (NORTH NODE PISCES)

*I*f you were born between these dates you have your South Node in Virgo:

Dec 29 1931—June 24 1933

July 27 1950—Mar 28 1952

April 20 1969—Nov 2 1970

Dec 3 1987—May 22 1989

June 22 2006—Dec 18 2007

With your South Node in Virgo you were ruled by

Mercury in your past life, so look to see where Mercury is in your chart—what house it's in—and what sign it's in as well. It's all part of the puzzle...

Virgo is able to see the ideal and is willing to make it become reality. You can analyze and intuit what needs to be done and you work, in one area of your life, to do it perfectly. That's where the trouble begins with Virgo: too much analyzing and perfectionism. You are called with this Nodal axis now to learn to trust in the process of life and to surrender your anxieties to a higher power. This is the call of your North Node in Pisces.

In a past life we could imagine you were being watched or observed and you had high expectations of yourself, and others did too. You could have been a doctor, priest, or skilled craftsperson—someone who was expected to be precise and perfect. There's also a good chance that you had healing abilities too as the Virgo/Pisces polarity is like the 6th and 12th house polarity and is related to the mind, body, spirit continuum.

. . .

In that past life there may have been a struggle about who you were, perhaps stressing and doubting about yourself. There may have been a lack of self-confidence and issues around duty guilt and shame. You were your worst enemy. You may have internalized inadequacy and sometimes even guilt— and you would have been the least guilty of all! But this is part of the past story that still may haunt you.

In this life now you are called to transcend boundaries by bringing the head and heart together and to bring an imaginative awareness into everything you do. You can relax and not demand from yourself that you play strictly by the Rules. Creativity and self expression is more important now than always doing the "right thing." Your Pisces North Node is calling you to gentle healing.

Ways You Might Sabotage Yourself and Your Relationships Unconsciously

Humility and pride are always an issue for Virgo. Sometimes it's as if you just can't find the right balance between the two—at times you can be too proud of yourself and your work and at other times you can be hit by a crippling lack of pride. You may fear to take a risk or do something different because you might not succeed. And not taking risks and not trying new things leads to lack of success, as well as the syndrome: "All work and no play makes Jack a dull boy."

With this Virgo/Pisces Nodal combination you sabotage yourself when you're not open to the deep psyche and the hints it sends you. You're meant delve into your psyche beyond the rational mind: explore your intuition as well as what music and the healing arts can offer you. You may have a natural talent in those areas you might not know about.

Your challenge in this life is to keep the ability to discriminate and analyze that has been developed in other lives but to combine these with compassion. Adjust your expectations to more realistic levels: don't fall into the default pattern of the critical judgmental person who finds nothing pleasing. If you relax your judgments you'll find that you are more loved than you realize.

In a former life, or in some ways in this life, there may be a tendency to still want to continue to do things "just right." And this perfectionism is a harsh standard to live up to it—in attempting to be perfect you inevitably fail; and thereby internalize a feeling of inadequacy or shame....this could also have come from the results of living under the ego-shattering impact of discipleship under an exacting master, guru, or person who had "power over you" (even sexual abuse). You may have had competitive siblings or demanding parents...or you may have been under the strict eye of someone older and more controlling--- or even a cultural system (such as Puritanism or Nazi-ism) that disempowered you in setting strict standards of behavior.

Having been the one who was duty-bound and played according to the 'Rules' in a former life (or earlier in this one) you now have the chance to relax your linear mind and move towards your heart's true desires. What is it you truly long for now? Is it love, beauty, imaginative creativity? Or is it simply the chance to relax your guard and take in the view from the mountaintop? Now you have the chance to unite the impulses of your head with those of your heart. You can dare to be gentle with yourself now, and dare to make mistakes, to be imperfect and to let some details go; being compassionate and forgiving with yourself as well as with others.

It's a good idea to practice getting out of unpleasant situations gracefully rather than being duty-bound or judgmental. You don't "have to be right" now or confrontational, and you can dare to use your intuition and take action even when you don't have all the answers. You don't have to over-analyze things any more. You don't have to struggle so much now to survive or evolve—instead you are called to move beyond "scarcity mentality" and a self-limiting place of "humble exactitude". Part of your soul-yearning in this life is to learn to simply trust in the process of life and to surrender your anxieties to a higher power. You are more loved than you realize.

. . .

So in love relationships, you will find "soul medicine" in the soft edges and accepting ways of your Pisces North Node. Compassionate, imaginative, inclusive, and—even boundary-less at times, this Pisces/Virgo axis calls for rounding the edges of your psyche so that you are neither critical of yourself or others.

Neptune rules Pisces, so all Neptunian activities are good for you...whether it be walking along the beach by the ocean, meditating, having a glass of wine, or playing imaginatively like a child. Love relationships are healing when they move away from the humble, disciplined and earth bound nature of Virgo to the realms where the head and the heart unite in the less discriminating waters of Pisces.

As you see, it's your compassion and intuition that will bring you success and satisfaction in this life. Simply by softening your attitude and doing what needs to be done with an accepting attitude you will find that you awaken that which you are yearning for, because it is already deep within your Soul! This Pisces/Virgo axis can create a magical life.

. . .

Gold in the shadow of this Node: You can solve almost any problem and you're willing to help others solve their problems, you have trustworthiness, and a touch of genius. A faithful lover.

Physical issues with the Virgo South Node could be around the skin and the intestines.

SOUTH NODE LIBRA (NORTH NODE ARIES)

*I*f you were born between these dates you have a South Node in Libra:

July 8 1930—Dec 28 1931

Jan 27 1949—July 26 1950

Aug 20 1967—April 19 1969

April 7 1986—Dec 2 1987

Dec 26 2004—June 21 2006

. . .

Do you remember how you feel when you've been trying too long—hours, days, weeks—to make everyone happy and get along? When you've had to watch what you said and did *constantly*? Well, put that into a lifetime and you have the Soul squelching habits of South Node Libra who obeyed all the rules and didn't have much fun. You likely were enmeshed in a relationship, family or clan where co-dependence was the norm and you barely knew what *you* really thought and felt.

Now your North Node in Aries calls you to be a spiritual warrior, to be an entrepreneur, to be an independent thinker and doer. You are a survivor—and your Mars ruled Aries North Node is a lovely energetic balance to your Venus ruled South Node.

The limitations of too-close enmeshed partnerships and relationships don't have to last for a lifetime. But those Libra South Node habits left unconscious trails in your psyche. Both Carl Jung and Sigmund Freud had these South Node points and when it came time for their relationship to end they both went into a tailspin. Freud had been looking for someone to mentor and Jung was mesmerized by his Elder's knowledge—but when they outgrew each other, leaving wasn't easy. Jung went into his now famous "confrontation with the unconscious" that lasted years, and Freud became not only enraged at Jung but beset by fits of fainting and other psychosomatic ailments. If they had followed their past life Libra patterns—the easier default pattern—life would have been simpler for both of them but they wouldn't have become as great as they did because of following their independent North Nodes.

So, the idea of "going along with things" and compromising behavior leads you into the shadows with this Nodal combination. But what about the gifts of this combo? Grace, empathy and a sense of humor also comes with this Venus ruled South Node. Because you were skilled at getting along with others and also because of the Libra inclination towards the arts and justice, you may have some hidden talents that surprise you...who knew you could paint so well? No one was surprised as much as you were when you became quite good at "the arts" with a minimal amount of work.

Ways You May Sabotage Yourself and Your Relationships Unconsciously

In Evolutionary astrology we look at the South Node with eyes that are biased to see what unfinished business, what blockage, what challenge was not met—either earlier in this life or in a former life. So, we read the South Node negatively. To read the "Venus ruled" Libra negatively can be hard, because there is so much charm and personality there. It's similar to saying "that nice person at the party wasn't really so nice after all." Too much niceness, too much 'trying to make the peace at any price', too much caring what the other person thinks and feels, can make a person appear like a chameleon. Why is there such a desire to please? What woundedness is under that need?

Enmeshment, co-dependence, and a subtle kind of opportunism and neediness are the worse traits of

Libra; no matter if it be the Sun, Moon or South Node. In the South Node position, the emotional nature "remembers" on a cellular level an original closeness and unity that is hoped for now, if not expected. Venus wants good relationships, harmony and beauty. Nothing wrong with that. Justice too, and credit for doing a good job. He/she wants to come up smelling like roses, and sometimes Venus bends the truth or takes radical risks to make their dreams come true.

So what is needed here? A healthy dose of its opposite: Mars. Venus needs the independent, assertiveness of its North Node of Aries to create the balance. When you have the South Node in Libra, there's too much of a default pattern here of the illusive or manipulative feminine—whether you are male or female, we all have our counter-sexual parts within us, and with Libra, you are going to have to assert, fight, survive, and carry the weight of the paradoxes of life on your shoulders. You need to get assertive. Your soul survival may depend on you not depending too much on other people.

As always there's a delicate crucial balance needed

between the opposites. This is the Libra/Aries, "I--Thou axis" the relationship balancing "see-saw" between me and you. There's great gold or goodness embedded in the South Node Libra, but if you're going to learn from this, take a look at how you "act-out" your relationships in your life, and how you respond to beauty. Are you nourishing yourself with "random acts of beauty" and loving kindness? Good, that's high Libra. Are you finding new ways to nourish your need for true relationships, or are you distracting or deceiving yourself and others? Libra likes the illusions and beauty of Neptunian fantasies, which are fine, but remember to honor the need for confrontation and assertion in your life. Venus needs Mars. The female and male parts of you are all there inside of you, just asking permission to express itself. "Androgyny" can be seen as a kind of wholeness.

When you're too nice for too long, and you're not truly feeling all that "niceness" you get sick. Or you lose your passion; your Soul. You may think you've been doing good because you never get mad and show your temper but with this Nodal combination it's deadly. You are called to your Aries North Node instincts: take a risk and have an adventure. Feel your courage! Conventional roles need to be left behind, for you are called to be a pioneer, an entrepreneur and the one who dares to break new ground.

It's a slippery slope for this Libra South Node when the world thinks you're just fine and yet you know that something is missing. You can slip into boredom and being boring. You can be doing all the right things and yet carry an unconscious chip on your shoulder and not know why. It may be because you're cheating yourself from going to the edge! Work a little harder at what you do, speak with more passion and honesty. Dare to show your vulnerable self and see what happens. Push a little more; look over the edge to see what's there. And then blaze a path for the rest of us. Your North Node in Aries is the path of the *Sacred Warrior* so that's the star you need to follow home. Look to see what sign Venus is in your chart and what house it is in…this will tell you some of how and where the past life drama was acted out.

. . .

Gold in the Shadow of this South Node: grace, empathy, humor, artistic talent, sensual and sexual power, diplomacy.

Physical issues with a South Node in Libra could be related to the kidneys, adrenals and hormones.

SOUTH NODE SCORPIO (NORTH NODE TAURUS)

Your South Node is in Scorpio if your birthday falls between these dates:

Dec 29 1928—July 7 1930

Aug 3 1947—Jan 26 1949

Feb 20 1966—Aug 19 1967

Sept 12 1984—April 6 1986

April 14 2002—Dec 25 2004

Having suffered from too much drama, trauma and

even tragedy in a former life you come into this world with an innate deep seriousness. There can be a tendency towards seeing the negative, the suspicious, or the darkness before realizing that you are safe and it's a sunny day. Some people with this South Node unconsciously go on the defense from birth and act like all is well and with an attitude of "isn't life grand" in order to hide a deep fear and lack of trust. Pollyanna was probably born with this Nodal axis. So you see that the Soul that incarnated on this axis can play it out by being overly serious and cautious or choose a pre-emptive positive persona that hides the fear and trauma of the past life story beneath a pleasing façade.

With your Venus ruled North Node in Taurus you've come into this life to regain a sense of trust in yourself and in your process of soul growth. You're called now to discover what I call the "Sacred in the Commonplace" and to know serenity.

Venus is the antidote for your Pluto ruled South Node in Scorpio. Your past Pluto ruled life brought you to the edge and back; you died and were reborn many times. You may have experienced the worst humanity knows; the extremes of evil and harshness. (Some of us born right after WWII may have lived and died through the worst of that war.)

And in waking from that dream/nightmare you may find yourself still fascinated by the dark side of life...but don't go there. That is the seduction of the Pluto ruled Scorpio South Node. You are called instead to Taurus: to find comfort and security in the world now. You are called to calm down and return to a life of the senses...to the world of Venus ruled Taurus. It will be important for you to gain emotional, financial and physical security in the world and not be led into the shadows of the world of an outsider.

Ways You May Sabotage Yourself or Your Relationships Unconsciously

Do you choose relationships with people who are soulful or fascinating but who aren't grounded in this reality? Who can't keep a job or who jump from one relationship to another? In choosing to be with them you are repeating your past life pattern and that kind of person won't help you to learn trust. You may live out that relationship pattern for awhile, but you'd be wise to really ponder your true values and needs. Are you thinking only in terms of the short term or simply not thinking at all? Perhaps limiting yourself to what you think is enticing/seductive/sexy?

You may think you don't turn away from honest self reflection but you still may be naive. You may respect others who show their vulnerabilities but you need to take care of your tender Self that has suffered much in the past. A drunken musician may have a golden hearted persona but if you live with him day after day you're likely going to see the flip side of narcissism and selfishness.

It's a good quality of this South Node to be able to see the shadow and the light in themselves and others. But when you live too long in the Plutonian shadows without taking the grounded steady steps towards self-sufficiency and independence you're setting yourself up for trouble. Part of your purpose this time around is to show yourself that you can be resourceful and use your own abilities to support yourself. Learn to trust yourself first and trust in others and Life will follow after. That's the best gift that Scorpio South Node folks can do and happens to be the first Commandment after all—to love oneself and one's God.

Because the South Node in Scorpio is ruled by Pluto, "Lord of the Underworld" and is the archetypal symbol of death and rebirth there has been a struggle to transform and be re-born like the phoenix. Somewhere in all that struggling has come an exhaustion and weariness of the spirit. There can be a soul weariness. You need to know again that life can be good.

Pluto is an intensely passionate planet, and the exhausting Scorpio storyline is often the price it costs to come into one's own power. But having your South Node here suggests that you can heal and regenerate yourself—and others—more skillfully than any other sign. Yet you can also be secretive, reflective, mysterious and sometimes revengeful or jealous. This South Node in Scorpio often reflects the journey of coming into one's own power the hard way. Somewhere in your psyche you know the dark side of life; the areas that are taboo, and the horrific tragedies that befall humans. Tragedies leave scars in their wake, and though you've had great courage to look and survive these times, there's a heaviness of spirit that often remains, as well as a suspiciousness and fear. This life is now one where you are being called to rethink your values, your priorities, and to allow the old ways of loving and being loved to "die and be reborn."

There's great gold in Scorpio's shadowy inheritance---it has a hard won wisdom and occult knowledge that can serve you well when used right. But as always with Scorpio, there can be a tendency to see the "glass as half empty rather than half full" because of an intuitive awareness of what wasn't "right" earlier in this life or in a former life. You may have paid too much attention to other people's business rather than our own. You were—or are--

the power behind the throne, or the one who "borrowed" another's values, glory, money or husband. Your own yearning may have brought on drama and melodrama.

Now there's a call to love and be loved from a different perspective. No more tragic love stories, no more battles for power, struggles for revenge, hidden agendas and all the stuff of great novels. Just peace. Negotiation. Serenity. That's the movement that is called for with a Scorpio Moon or South Node. Your Soul needs a rest from trauma and melodrama—and you deserve it. There's no need to sabotage or save in the realm of love, but instead to find ways that life can be sweeter and easier with those you love, and that comfort itself and the simple joys in life are often what makes life worth living.

Look to see what sign Pluto is in on your chart and what house it falls in...that will take you further on the road to understanding your past life story. Look to Venus too, she's there to soothe and move you towards the Light.

. . .

Gold in the Shadow of this South Node: Healing powers, honesty, depth of vision that doesn't shy away from the truth, charisma, humor, sexiness.

Physical issues with a South Node in Scorpio could be around the reproductive organs.

SOUTH NODE SAGITTARIUS
(NORTH NODE GEMINI)

*I*f your birthday falls between these dates your South Node is in Sagittarius:

April 17 1927—Dec 28 1928

Dec 14 1945—Aug 2 1947

Aug 26 1964—Feb 19 1966

Mar 17 1983—Sept 11 1984

Oct 13 2001—Apr 13 2003

As a South Node Sagittarian you have been on a

philosophic quest in a former life and have accumulated a spiritual "mountain-top" kind of knowledge from your past life and are now being called to bring what you know into action in the "marketplace of life." Your wisdom was of the high philosophic variety and was likely to have had blinders on it as well; it was true only up to a point. You edited out life's complexities and made colossal mistakes. Yet you were a true believer in your Faith and could have died nobly for your beliefs. Now you need to brush shoulders with the common man and acquire new experiences to deepen and to communicate a wider breath of knowledge.

For you Jupiter ruled Sagittarians, being able to communicate skillfully is really important, because in the past you may not have done it well. You may have had a self-convincing philosophy of life but you often had "foot in mouth" disease due to your lack of empathy. Now when I say you are called to learn communication, part of that is to learn to really *hear* what another person is saying; with their hearts as well as their lips.

. . .

Sagittarius, ruled by Jupiter, is the largest planet of the zodiac, and reflects the archetypes of the gypsy, the scholar and the arm-chair philosopher. This sign as a South Node suggests that your 'largeness' in a former life didn't always serve you well. There was an ego and confidence which likely came from lineage or entitlement rather than your working your way up to the top of the mountain. You traveled widely perhaps and even read widely, but too much of your knowledge was funneled down to fit into what you already believed. Open-mindedness and humility were not your strengths. You didn't want to learn what didn't fit into your idea of "how it all is."

Having suffered from Jupiterian too-muchness in a former life you are now likely finding yourself with more humble opportunities to become a self-made person who has worked towards success from the bottom up. You can now go into the world and truly learn from your new experiences for you are becoming street savvy. This is your North Node in Mercury ruled Gemini. Your life questing has come full circle from the abstract to the Real as tested in the marketplace of life. You have the challenge (and opportunity) to really understand the common person now and you could become a bridge-maker between people. And if you combine your earnest South Node Sagittarian *quest-ing* (questioning) with your North Node Gemini *openness* to new experiences you could become not only a Truth Teller but a person who could unite the opposites and bring peace when there was none before—you can become a bridge maker between people. Or you may fail at this task. (This is Donald Trump's South Node sign.)

Ways You May Sabotage Yourself or Your Relationships unconsciously

Although you are big spirited and caring, this South Nodes also carries traits of impatience, anger, and attention seeking behavior; even some unpredictability when you've kept your thoughts and feelings closed down for too long. You make a great storyteller, but like the Irish, you may tend to exaggerate your stories. Nothing wrong with that really but what can be a problem for you is "foot in mouth" disease: saying the first thing that comes to mind rather than thinking of how it will be received. Tactfulness isn't one of your strong points but most people overlook it because of your generous big-heartedness. You didn't meant to "say that exactly" and you can usually talk your way out of those situations. Be a little mindful about risk taking too, because your ruling planet Jupiter is not one to be cautious, and sometimes that's just what is called for.

Because of an unconscious addiction to certainty, or at least *the hope* for certainty, you may still seek familiar roads to travel rather than daring to break new ground. When your partner wants to go to a party, the café, or hang out with "different people" you'd be wise to go along. You are challenged to be non-judgmental and to risk lacking in self-confidence at times. *Certain aspects of your life need to de-construct so it can be re-constructed in a new way.* Allow yourself to break new ground.

If you can embrace this openness to new experiences life will open you up to becoming not only a phenomenal Truth teller but someone who communicates without even speaking; by their craft, their art, their ability to heal and in the "act of loving" in relationships. You have so much to give, but keep an eye on your reluctance or resistance to the New. Your North Node in Gemini is the sign of the Twins and it beckons you to conversation and honest dialog with everyone.

You don't need to go to extremes as you may have done in your past life "questing" but you do need to open the door to the collision of the opposites in your life, which is one of the hardest things we have to bear psychically. It will be your ability to find the "Third Way" as you handle and synthesize the tension of the opposites that will create your genius. Carl Jung wrote about this inner alchemical work frequently—activate the gold in your Mercury ruled South Node and check it out!

And look to the sign and house placement of Jupiter in your chart to add to your past life story. Was it in your 7th house of partnerships indicating that marriage was the arena on which some of this took place, or was in the 10th house of career? You may want to see where—what house-- the North Node and Mercury, the ruler of Gemini, falls in your chart too. It is all like a puzzle or personal Zen koan for you to ponder in this life.

Gold in the Shadow of this South Node: Your innate understanding that we are all on a "Quest" like the main character in a movie, you expect obstacles and take on life optimistically. Good natured-ness, optimism, and soulfulness.

Physical problems for those with Sagittarius South Node could be with the hips, and with blood sugar problems or weight.

SOUTH NODE CAPRICORN (NORTH NODE CANCER)

*I*f you were born between these dates your South Node is Capricorn:

Oct 27 1925—Apr 16 1927

May 12 1944—Dec 13 1945

Dec 24 1962—Aug 25 1964

Sept 25 1981—Mar 16 1983

Apr 10 2000—Oct 12 2001

Capricorn, ruled by Saturn, can be a stern teacher.

With this South Node you likely were forced to survive by putting one foot ahead of another stoically for many years. There could have been relentless pressures and duties that simply had to be done. And you did what needed to be done, while also learning how to live with solitude in your Soul. You developed self-denial and character in a harsh environment, and likely you didn't complain. But your stiff upper lip took a toll on your Soul.

In this life your primary job is to heal from these austerities, which may have been repeated in the first part of this life. With a North Node in the Moon ruled Cancer you are called to cry a few tears, to soften and to know the joy of the gentler aspects of life. Cultivating a sense of humor may be one of those tasks, as well as developing friendships and relationships that can sustain you and bring you out of a hermit like stance. You never had that before.

You don't need to be famous or even make your mark on this world; you simply need to heal and soften. There is a part of you that has shut yourself down so much emotionally that you barely know what it is to deeply feel anymore. When you prioritize the demands of "sheer practicality" it can be a way of slipping back into not being in touch with feelings. It's now time to let go of your "inner Eeyore" and allow the lunar or looney side of you out. The Moon rules your North Node in Cancer so it's as if you are given a cosmic permission slip to be as wacky and silly as you want, full moon or not. But in truth, the gold in your Capricorn South Node has integrity and a sense of responsibility that will balance the lunar side of your personality.

Ways You May Sabotage Yourself or Your Relationships Unconsciously:

As a Capricorn South Node person you will not rush into romance or close friendship with just anybody. You are attracted to qualities like dignity and the old-fashioned trait of "good breeding." You look for substance over style and you're willing to work for what you want. But how many people can see the strongly erotic and even hedonistic side of you? Not many; they see the serious good-natured side of you without realizing that you are very discriminating with potential marriage partners, but…others? Well, be careful, because you could hurt some very sensitive people out there. You have a wonderful sense of humor and an ability to withstand the winters of life, but realize that others may not be as strong as you. You are a survivor, and there's no sense of leaving a trail of broken hearts after you…

Despite your strength, you have the planets Saturn and the Moon ruling your Nodal axis. This can hint that there can be a tendency to slip into depression or illness that has its roots deep in a constricted unhappy past. And depression in all its forms, particularly the inward turning lack of self-expression, can cripple your ability to savor the sweetness of friendship or partnership. The prescription for you is to allow others into your heart and dare to commit to people and relationships. You are more loved than you realize and you don't need to see yourself as the strong loner or the uncommitted bachelor.

. . .

Look to where Saturn is in your chart, what house, and sign it's in to give you a deeper clue to your past life story and look to the sign and house of your Moon—and as we go along with this technique we'll also be adding other planetary influences as well. Follow the trail and use that highly intuitive Cancer North Node to help you!

Physical issues for those with a South Node in Capricorn might include problems with the bones, such as arthritis, or with the knees.

Gold in the Shadow of the South Node Capricorn: You know how to succeed in the world and you have integrity combined with a strong work ethic. When you choose to let it out, you have a great sense of humor.

SOUTH NODE AQUARIUS (NORTH NODE LEO)

*I*f you born between these dates, then your South Node is in Aquarius:

Apr 24 1924—Oct 25 1925

Nov 22 1942—May 11 1944

June 11 1961—Dec 23 1962

Jan 13 1980—Sept 24 1981

Oct 21 1998—April 9 2000

. . .

With your South Node in Aquarius you hold the archetypes of the outsider, the rebel, or exile in your

past. Ruled by the planet Uranus, there was a feeling of "me" vs "them" in a former life and it may have been a very mean battle indeed. There could have been an experience of torture or persecution or simply the pain of being unheard, even when you knew you were innocent and right. You may have suffered from dissociation; a retreat into an inner world that kept you isolated from others.

In this life you are called to build bridges rather than inner or outer walls. You are called to speak your truth now, with warm self-confidence and to "come in from the cold" as the Joni Mitchell song goes…there is no longer a need to protect yourself from "authorities" or others who you feared or hated. There's a certain cool self-protectiveness that can still linger in the psyche of the South Node Aquarius person that benefits by the warmth of the North Node sign Leo. Allow yourself to relax your guard and speak from your heart; not your anger or some vague uneasiness in your Soul. Those times are over. Now it's time to play!

Earlier in this life or in a former life you were living on the sidelines watching others interact on center stage. You felt exiled, even if you weren't. Now its time to engage yourself actively—be creative with a paintbrush, your children or simply with how you live each day. Color outside the lines of your everyday life and rejoice in the results.

When you talk it's important for you to speak more from your heart than from your head. There's a tendency to be so objective and occasionally aloof that you can lose touch with the feeling based world you live in. (A presence of many planet in earth and water can certainly off-set this, so always the whole chart needs to be considered.) But still there can be painful half-forgotten soul-memories that can arise in moods you don't understand.

The North Node in Leo is the perfect antidote for this. Leo rules the heart and you've come into this world to be seen and accepted and to feel the joy of knowing love. Dare to give your talents and gifts to the world. Don't always wait for others to ask you —take the initiative yourself.

Ways You May Sabotage Yourself or Your Relationships Unconsciously:

Aquarius sensitivities are coupled with a self - confidence born of not worrying too much about other's opinions and this self-assuredness can make you very attractive—along with the fact that you usually love to talk and enjoy making the other person happy. You can also be thoughtful and quite a romantic at times. There can be a tendency to lead from the head rather than the heart, as well as an unpredictability and detachment about you that's hard for others to understand. These are qualities of your planetary ruler, Uranus.

Although you tend towards being open-minded and humanitarian there can also be a stubborn and extremist part of your nature. You don't need to change who you are—and you know that—but practicing saying "I love you" more would be a wonderful habit to consider. Because you carry the imprint of the outsider on your Soul you may have developed a protective mechanism of judging yourself or others harshly. As you release this tendency you could practice forgiveness and letting your funny bone out! Humor acknowledges the dark side of life with a detached and ironic perspective (a gift of Aquarius.)

You sabotage yourself when you get too serious and step back from others...your Soul instead yearns to come forward now, to take chances, to see life as a game worth playing—simply because it's fun and a challenge. When you follow "your bliss" as the mythologist Joseph Campbell once said, you engage the best of your North Node Leo potential for shining and sharing; you engage your generous heart.

With the South Node in Aquarius you would be advised not to engage in stern and "objective" practices such as Zen Buddhism but rather to do inner reflection on what makes you laugh, cry or rage? You really have something to say or express in this life. The key for you is to be mindful of how you communicate to others; if you have the warm Leo empathy as a base you will find yourself deeply accepted and loved. Chuck the cool "above it all" attitude and come join the family of man. You've earned it!

Physical issues with a South Node Aquarius might be around the ankles and also with the body's electrical system.

Gold in the Shadow of South Node Aquarius: You're a natural conversationalist and some of you border on being genius because you have the ability to think "out of the box." You are charismatic, with an ability to see all sides of an issue and play fair. You're a good friend and a person who may surprise others.

SOUTH NODE PISCES (NORTH NODE VIRGO)

*I*f you were born between these dates your South Node would be Pisces:

Aug 24 1922—Apr 23 1924

May 25 1941—Nov 21 1942

Dec 16 1959—June 10 1961

July 6 1978—Jan 12 1980

Jan 26 1997—Oct 20 1998

With a South Node in Neptune ruled Pisces you

came into this life with a sense of magic and a keen imagination. There may also be a psychic sensitivity and a natural spirituality whether or not you choose to give it any formal name. Yet we always read the South Node from the point of view of what you didn't get right and what you suffered from in a former life. And for you there was a loss of Self where you perceived the world as if from a dream state. Disillusionment wore you down.

There could have been many reasons for that disillusioned Self: you may have been the victim of a crime, or have been ill or abused. Or you may have allowed yourself to be trapped in a soul cage like a *too strict adherence to rules* of a monastery or nunnery. Or you could have been in a family role that restricted you so much that you became your "role" as mother, sick child, artist, or over-worked father. Trying to regain your sense of Self you may have become too self-absorbed and subjective, and you may have compensated with food or drink or simply fantasies that took you away from your confinement. There could have been addiction and confusion. There seemed no way out or in. There is also the possibility that you may have been a mystic and become One with God. But there was an imbalance: you often did a spiritual bypass on an emotional problem; on life.

Now in this life you are called to regain that sense of Self that you lost. You are called to find joy again. There are many ways to do that, but one simple way that your North Node in Virgo suggests is by being of service to others in a way that you choose; you gladly offer your gifts and abilities because you want to do so. *Giving and receiving love* can heal your Soul. You can see the Ideal now and you are willing to work to make it a reality. That's the key word here; Reality. And reality isn't always glamorous or mystical but it can be very good.

To go for your best, you'll need to plan and strategize as you set your priorities, and to pay attention to details in a way you never did before. You can use that gift for analyzing situations that your North Node Virgo gives you to see clearly what needs to be done. And it's not always about the service to others, it's about that process of focusing and becoming competent that enables you to bring your dreams into reality. It's time to regain your faith again that life itself can be good. God may be in the details for you, and those details can be very sweet if you have the heart to see them, and you do.

Ways You May Sabotage Yourself or Your Relationships Unconsciously:

You may have a tendency to moodiness and escapism which can sabotage the ability for you to have a rich life, and make it hard for others to reach you. Common pitfalls for this South Node include addictions of all kinds and a periodic loss of faith in Life. Like your symbol of the Piscean fish who sometimes have to travel upstream on their way home, you too are not without the necessity for hard work and effort. And when you're feeling optimistic, you will willingly work for what you believe. But don't be too upset if you have to keep looking hard to find that person or work situation that you can love and devote yourself too. Be patient in your process.

. . .

Meanwhile, make a note to yourself keep participating in life and get involved! Don't sink into a dream world waiting for the right moment. When you don't look beyond your inner world to *skillfully* participate in life, you sink into a dull dream of life that's bound by illusions and other people's expectations--then you lose that cherished love that comes from serving others and the world in *your unique way*.

Another way to say this is don't get lazy. Become disciplined: become a "disciple" to that which you love. When you follow your unique path that way you won't be tempted to slip into addictions or conspiracy theories or self-centeredness. There is a Sweet Reality out there that calls you to follow your dreams; to create for yourself the world you want.

The Virgo/Pisces axis also has potential talents as healers and with music. Many famous musicians over the years have had strong variations of the Virgo-Pisces signature in their charts, perhaps because the Pisces part of their psyche can "hear" the music and the Virgo part can both analyze and discipline itself to write the notes down or set them to memory. Paul McCartney has this Nodal axis. There's a lot of gifts with this Nodal combination but they must be retrieved by you from your deep psyche.

Look to where Neptune is in your chart—what house it's in and what sign. Look to what planets may be conjunct, opposing or squaring your Nodes. And look to Mercury as well as the ruler of Virgo. This is the Mercury that is skillful, cunning and wise.

Physical issues for those with a Pisces South Node

might be around the feet and emotional health.

Gold in the Shadow of this South Node: Creativity, imaginative nature, heartfelt, intuitive if not psychic, a visionary.

THE HOUSES: WHERE IS IT HAPPENING IN MY CHART?

*N*ow you need to add on the House placement to your South Node Sign. Each of the twelve houses describes a particular area of life and this will be described in each section. This information will fill in your story quite a bit. Where was the action? We look to the "houses" in a chart to see where the story of the Nodes was being lived out. Was it in your career (10th house) or in your family and home (4th house)?

There are different house systems, but in my lineage of teachers they have all used the Placidus house system. Most evolutionary astrologers believe it is the best house system for this type of Soul-centered astrology. I truly don't think a "case" can be made for any one system, so I'm not going to even try. And along the same line, I use the Mean Node as opposed to the True Node although they are only about a degree apart. The Nodes "wobble" in space making them difficult to pinpoint exactly, so using either the Mean or True Node is acceptable. *However, when a Node is close to another sign or house, then it's on the cusp and it's necessary to look at both signs and houses that are being touched.*

And when we look at the South Node houses remember we read them negatively, or in their lower octave of expression. The house was about where the suffering or unfinished business was happening in a previous life. And *remember that the past life story repeats the same way in the signs and houses, so we are also talking about your life now.*

If the South Node is in the First House:

The first house generally describes you—your personality—in fuller detail than the Ascendent— particularly if you have planets there. Where was the action? In the transformation of your personality. And the flavor of the first house, ruled by Mars, reflects the pattern of the independent Aries-like hero/heroine who is on a quest to know who they are and to move assertively out into the world. Aries is like the spiritual warrior; the one who is honing their courage in this life...so that Aries/Mars *undertone* is part of your first house no matter what sign occupies that house.

What we have here may be an exaggerated sense of independence or issues around freedom or lack of it. There could be excessive fear or worry—something which kept you away from committed interaction with your career or with another person. There could have been shyness or concern for the needs of others, or even a sense that others were "enemies" and it may have been true. Whether or not there had been courage and assertive action in the past, the compensating challenge for you now is of bringing significant others and partners into your life. That's the 7th house where your North Node is placed. There's a move here from past life solo behavior and independence to embracing inter-dependence with others.

If the South Node is in the Second House:

The second house is the arena of your personal resources, your values and your money or lack of it. That's where the action was; that's where the essence of the story was played out. As a South Node placement it could also mean a lack of self-confidence in a former life. The natural undertone of the second house is reflected in its planet and its sign: Venus and Taurus. It reflects a pattern of concern around survival issues; physically, emotionally and financially. There has been a mark of insecurity and fear left over even if you were doing well in those areas! You may have felt disempowered in a former life, and the basic needs and comforts of life took on large importance.

With a South Node here you somehow missed your calling and didn't carry through on the things that were important to you. So now, there's a need to really look at your values and with your compensating North Node function in the 8th house you are called to take risks and do deep inner work. You are meant to get intimately involved with others and to create a pragmatic philosophy of life that is rooted in confidence and a deep understanding of life.

If the South Node is in the Third House:

The Third house is the area of life that rules how we communicate, and our relationships with our siblings. This was where it was happening for you. The third house natural ruler is the planet Mercury, and the sign of Gemini. This is the undertone for this house no matter what South Node Sign you may have here. With this Gemini undertone we see that there were problems related to how you talked, how you listened—or didn't listen, and how you related to others. Relationships with your siblings may be of karmic importance as well.

If we were to think in images there's a feeling of a fast-talking quick acting person here; perhaps a comedian or a pickpocket, or a jobless person pleading with another for an opportunity to work. Maybe a con artist. The talk is fast, maybe clever, and a bit opportunistic or glib. And of course, this tends to become your default pattern in this life when you're not careful.

The evolutionary intention is towards the North Node in the 9th house which has a mountain-top vision asking you to slow down and reflect, create a plan and look deep into what you really want. There may also be unresolved issues with brothers and sisters and situations from your early childhood.

Communication is the key word for this Nodal axis, and especially with your brothers and sisters. You can get trapped in an unending conversation that goes on with them for a lifetime…even when you're not speaking with them. Same conversation. Karmic issues with siblings are a mystery—why did we choose them or why did they choose us to reincarnate with? Did we come together now to learn and grow more? Thoughtful and skillful conversation is the key here.

If the South Node is in the Fourth House:

The Fourth house is the area of your life that rules your family of origin, your home, and even how you see the mythology of your life. It relates to your physical house now and in the past, and I often think of it as being the 3 h's: home, heart and hearth. The Moon is the ruling planet and Cancer is the ruling sign, so the *undertone* for this house has the lunar Cancerian nature to it no matter what your South Node sign is.

You may have prioritized family before, and you may still be doing that, but your North Node in the 10th house urges you to focus more on being out in the world and your career. The particular challenge with this house is to learn to honor the fluctuations and moods of lunar Cancerian nature while taking purposeful action in the world.

In your past life there may have been unquestioning loyalty to your family despite an entanglement of conflicting emotions. The family engulfed and defined you in a prior life so it would be good for you now to look at your family karmic inheritance and to know the good, bad and ugly on the family tree. Hopefully you can then take more of what you want and let the rest be. Your life, your goals, and the mission in your life now is more important than the quiet comforts of home, which may hold some Soul-stifling karma.

~

If the South Node is in the Fifth House:

The Fifth house describes the area of life having to do with your creativity, your love affairs, the things you do for pleasure and children. The sign associated with this house is Leo with its ruler being the Sun. The soul-purpose of Leo relates to having an open and generous heart, but many of us know its downside being that that it can present as too much "about me" and a "showing off" quality. Leo can also get maligned for its sometimes bossy ways and sense of entitlement, even when they aren't trying to do that.

In a past life a person with this placement may have been involved with a creative life; and who knows —touches of that can flower again in this life. But reading it negatively, there can also be a possibility of addictions and compulsions around the creativity and around what one does for pleasure. There is great creativity here but in the past the energy flowed backwards and inward to the self rather than outward to benefit humanity.

There can also be fears and insecurities about having children, or simply with one's children now, hinting that in the past life there were problems here. You could have broken "the rules of society" relating to sexuality and having children and suffered from that. And even your pleasures may have been the source of some pain.

In this life your 5th house South Node tends towards subjectivity, and so you are called to its polarity: the Eleventh house. This way is about being more objective, and to take the long view of things and to think strategically. You are also called to be more discerning in your friends and behavior; who is your tribe really? Have you networked to move beyond your default friends who may no longer be on the same page with you anymore? Have you considered moving away from the compulsive side of pleasures, of creativity, and even in the way your raise your children? Only you know how the Fifth House South Node may have touched your life and how old habits that you may have carried over from a previous life no longer need to burden your life now. Did you fall in love or lust too early and get pregnant as a teenager? Or make too quick decisions such as joining the military or some corporation and then realize that it was soul depleting? It takes awhile to move away from the slippery slope of South Node behavior but we all have them, and we are all able to turn around mid-stream and head for the North! Your 11th house North Node with its Aquarian/Uranus undertones will guide you to think differently and to find where you belong in this world.

If the South Node is in the Sixth House:

With your South Node placement in the house that is naturally ruled by the sign of Virgo and the planet Mercury, you were bound in the past by issues around duty, responsibilities, and perhaps servitude. It may have been voluntary or involuntary. The voluntary paths of discipleship and apprenticeship are also part of this placement. And, there may still be a habit or compulsion to be a workaholic or to be known as the one who worries a great deal and takes care of what must be done. Humility and pride were issues that plagued you in the past and may still linger on.

Now it's time to let that go and create more balance in your life; leaving some of the work and responsibilities to another person. You have earned

North Node gifts from the 12th house that has a Piscean undertone of magic, spirituality, and imagination. The 6th and 12th houses are on the mind/body/spirit axis and although you may have suffered from poor health in a former life you may now find yourself with a gift of healing yourself and others. Some people may also have unexplored gifts around music due to the Virgo/Pisces undertone that has been a mark of musicianship for ages.

No matter what sign your South Node is in with this 6th house placement, know that you are meant to now be an explorer of the deep psyche. You are called to learn the sacred subtle arts of life and to allow your head and heart to unite in this life. Sometimes people with Nodes on this axis find they enjoy doing two things in life more than just one; you might enjoy being an accountant by day and a musician in the evening, or a massage therapist and a painter. Marry your intuitive and heart promptings with your keen intellect to create a good life for you this time around.

If the South Node is in the Seventh House:

With the South Node in the house of marriage and partnerships and ruled by the planet Venus you were familiar with this side of life. In fact, the default tendency in the past life was to be totally defined by relationship so that you descended into becoming a role rather than a person. You lost yourself in the gilded cage of partnerships.

Ruled by the sign Libra, the undertone for your 7th house placement is one of soul-numbing enmeshment with another. This doesn't mean now that you shouldn't partner with someone but it does mean that you are now called to not be afraid of separation and even some enlightened self-centeredness.

Your North Node placement, and the antidote for this South Node is in the Mars ruled sign of Aries in the First House. The Mars/Aries/First House is self-assertive, and is always learning courage. It will make an effort to go first; to pave the way for the rest of us. This may be hard to do in the first part of life, but as you combine the sign of your South Node with this house placement in the 7th, you will find that heeding too closely to rules of justice, reason, and "getting along" to avoid trouble may still put you into a deadening attempt to please and accommodate. Don't do it!

Now you are being called to let conventional roles and habits give way to a more exciting, truthful and passionate nature. For you there is a yearning for the adrenaline rush of new beginnings and you learn to see fresh possibilities and new ideas as you follow the tendencies of your North Node first house placement. Give yourself permission not to follow through on every last detail. And speak the truth even when it's raw. Like in the fairytale about the Emperor with no clothes on you are the one to tell him the truth! And there are no social niceties with that one.

If the South Node is in the Eighth House:

This house placement has the undertone of the sign of Scorpio with its ruler Pluto; Lord of the Underworld. No matter what sign your South Node is, it will still carry the Scorpio past life signature of drama, trauma and intensity. Most likely there will have been tragedy as well, and whether you were the misguided perpetuator of the tragedy or the victim is hard to say. Often they are entwined, but some astrologers look to see if there are conjunctions of hard planets with the South Node as inclining perpetrating the drama and hard planets squaring or opposing it tend more toward being the "victim." By hard planets I mean Mars and Pluto especially.

Either way there is a carry-over in this life of deep wounding, fear, and anxiety. There has been something extreme in the past and such experiences don't leave their grip on the Soul easily. The healing for you in this life will be to regain your self-confidence and to have faith that life can be good, and that you are "good." You need to embrace your second house Venus ruled Taurus to ground you in the beautiful and sacred things in this life. Venus heals Pluto. Love heals wounds.

This South Node placement has great gifts in its shadowy inheritance—it has a hard won knowledge or wisdom that can serve you if used right. Astrologers and those interested in psychic matters often have resources here in the 8th house. With this placement however, you may have paid too much attention in the past life to other people's business rather than our own. You might have been the power behind the throne, or the one who 'borrowed' another's values, glory, money or husband. Now you are called to mind your own business and prove yourself to yourself—regain your self-confidence by creating a body of work or "a life" that is meaningful to you. Find where the joyful and safe place is to be, and relish all you're becoming.

If the South Node is in the Ninth House:

With the South Node here you have an undertone of the sign of Sagittarius and the planet Jupiter no matter what sign your South Node may be in. You will want to synthesize the meaning of your Sign here with the meaning of this house, knowing that the house placement tells us a lot about what arena of life your Nodes played out upon.

For you, your belief system in your last life shaped your existence. You lost a sense of "grounded-ness" in your instincts and commonsense because you were blinded by your faith and your zeal. You earnestly searched for Truth and may have had a great education and traveled widely but you didn't have an open mind. Everything you learned funneled into a belief system that was not curious for new information. You edited out life's complexities and nuances; you didn't want to hear that the world was round not flat. You knew it was flat because you had sailed far and wide.

With the South Node in the Ninth house, journeys and immigration may have been part of your life. You may have suffered and died on one of these journeys, and sadly your God didn't save you. Or you may have been part of the Crusades, or part of the Puritans sailing to America. You believed you were right and you may have allowed religion and a repressive morality to guide your decisions.

In this life now you are called to open up to new ways of thinking and being. You are being asked to be curious and follow through on those curiosities. Your North Node in the Third House calls you to sharpen your communication skills and to tell your stories, full of new information and delight. Let your world expand and don't retreat when you approach mystery. You don't need to travel widely in this life, although you can if you like. You are simply called to be a keen observer and student of Life and you can do that in your own neighborhood; that's a North Node Third tenet. You could be like Emily Dickenson who barely left her house but she could glean so much poetry by simply observing herself and the world around her. Inner questing can be at home or in the marketplaces of the world, but for you now, it's meant to expand any places of smallness, judgementalism and woundedness still in your Soul.

If the South Node is in the Tenth House:

This South Node placement is ruled by the planet Saturn and the sign Capricorn. So the *undertone* of your South Node Sign will have Capricorn qualities to it such as integrity, ambition, seriousness, leadership and the damage to the Soul caused by too much investment in a public or prominent role. Think of how much doctors and politicians sacrifice in their personal life to do their role in the world. Yes, power and status came along with this placement, but there was suffering and lessons not learned.

Your North Node in the Fourth House is calling you Home; both inner and outer. You are called to deep reflection on the "story of your life" and in making a home that is a safe refuge in the world. Having suffered a loss of soul somewhere out there in the world being 'somebody' you now are called to relax your ambitious nature just enough so that you carry heart into all that you do. Take care of yourself and your family. Be at home and don't get caught in a soul cage of status and propriety. You'd be missing something if you did…and freedom is one of them.

This doesn't mean that you can't use the gifts from your past life experience; you can reach for the "gold" in your innate knowing of how to survive in the world, and how to make meaning and to be of service in the world. This is good. You were on the stage of the world in the last life, and it can still be a comfortable place for you to be. But with your South Node there, realize that it has traps for you. Your public persona cries for time alone or with family and close friends. It needs time when it doesn't have to self-promote and jockey for position. You've earned prominence in your last life, you're now heading to nurture and heal the home spaces of the heart.

If the South Node is in the Eleventh House:

The Eleventh house is known primarily for its association with groups and friends, and it's very possible that you lost your sense of Self and individuality within a group. It could have been the military, a nunnery or even a cultural movement that you got swept up in. Ruled by the sign of Aquarius and the planet Uranus, we learn a little more. You may have been deeply involved in a group but it somehow turned against you. Perhaps you lost faith in part of the "tribe" you were in but couldn't find a way to honorably get out. You may have become an outsider within the group; but still you preserved. And suffered.

With your North Node house placement being in the fifth house, and ruled by the planet Leo, you are called to personal self expression in this life. Step out of the group and let yourself shine on your own! And take personal risks—have the love affair, have a child, express yourself creatively and playfully. That's all fifth house territory. This Nodal axis wants you to get personal—it doesn't need to get philosophical or political and talk about saving humanity—you've done that before. How about saving just one child at a time? And maybe that child could just be your inner child that's been neglected for awhile.

You'll want to move away from the 11th house propensities towards aloofness, objectivity, detachment and avoiding confrontations. In this life you can allow yourself to be "a character." Exercise your funny bone, and let yourself be known as having a generous heart. In the past life you've likely worked for others, so in this life, it is indeed all about you and that's the way it should be!

If the South Node is in the Twelfth House:

With your South Node here there's an *undertone* of the sign of Pisces and the planet Neptune, no matter what your South Node sign is. The placement of your SN here is significant because its hints that you suffered terrible loss and grief, or confinement in a hospital or institution in a prior life—and this mood may be the "emotional hangover" from the previous life. It doesn't mean that you will carry this with you now in this life, but that you learned some lessons from this tough placement of your South Node story.

Another twelfth house possibility is that you may have been part of a religious institution or mystical society in the past. You may have gained power and strong beliefs from that connection but often there remains karmic memories of misuse of power, or deprivation and pain in the body. These conditions could have caused you to seek relief in alcohol or drugs or even total immersion in God—or perhaps you lost it all together in that life and ended up institutionalized. It's all in the realm of possibility. And that's all in the past. The Neptunian confusion and yearning is giving way to the Mercurial and Virgo delights of living in this world of grounded Reality. You can now manage to move through this life in a skillful manner more than most.

With your North Node in the 6th house you are meant to come back into your body and take good care of it this time around. The 12th and 6th houses are on the body/mind/spirit continuum so what you do in one of those areas of your life will affect the others.

You may also find yourself with mentors and teachers around you; this is excellent as you benefit from being mentored and mentoring others.

Discipleship and lineage is part of this house placement.

Because the sixth house is also about service, you benefit when you are in service to others. This could be teaching or healing or crafting an object of beauty. There's a lot to heal from the past life house placement and self-care and care for others are now priorities. As you help others you are truly helping yourself.

PULLING IT ALL TOGETHER:
FOLLOWING THE TRAIL

*T*his is the chapter you may want to read in the morning with a cup of tea or coffee...and pen and paper as well. Think of yourself again as a spiritual detective gathering clues and you don't want to eliminate any possibilities till you see it all on the table.

It will be important for you to think of every piece of information you're gathering so far as clues and filters. Don't throw out anything in this alchemical stew. Let it all marinate in your psyche. Let all the possibilities of your journey come to you intuitively as well as strategically: write down the sign of your South Node, the house it's in, the planet that rules that South Node and where it is....and then add the juicy hints of the planets that may align themselves in some way to the South Node.

After pondering the qualities of those clues with pen and paper, write down the sign and house placement of the North Node. It too, is a part of the story although it's more the remedy or prescription for the ailments of the South Node parable.

Then with your notes on paper you'll need to let this marinate in your psyche for a few hours or days and then come back to it when your intuitive mind is open. You may come to this with faint intimations of that "forgotten dream of a previous life" and what it may entail. You've suffered the emotional hangover from it in your childhood dreams as well as in the circumstances of your early life. But now we're going to add some insights into that. Not biographical facts, but the Soul's story.

Try it now: write down the *sign* of your South Node and the *house description* of where the South Node lies in your chart. This takes a little mental alchemy to blend these, but after looking at those descriptions in this book, ponder your life story. Really look at it through the lens of this filter. This is a first pass at this, and I'll want you to come back to this later as well, but again, it needs to marinate in your deep psyche.

Then look at the *planetary ruler of the South Node and follow its trail.* For example, if your South Node is Libra and therefore ruled by Venus, then look to see what house Venus is in, and what sign Venus is in. That can resonate in your story. Is that Venus making aspects? Write it down, and add that to your detective work.

Then look to see if the South Node has any planets *conjunct.* These all work together to give you an idea of the character you were in a past life. It describes you then. Write down those characteristics.

Now look to see if there's any planets *opposing* the South Node (they would be conjunct the North Node) and you read these planets negatively as what opposed you in your past life. This was the *brick wall of reality you were up against.* This is what afflicted you then and could have been a person or a situation that you just couldn't get around. And just as the North Node is always read positively, you can also look at those very same planets as now being a positive influence! They can help you along if you use their higher octave of expression. For example, if Mars opposed your South Node in the past and you were up against violence, in this life now you can learn to use assertiveness skillfully and avoid violent confrontations.

Then look to see if there are any planets *square* to your South Node. This is also what afflicted you in a former life, and is a very important clue, as it also points to what my mentor, Steven Forrest, calls *"the skipped step."* Look at the description of that planet, and know that you have to come to terms with what afflicted you in the past, and that you are challenged to live out the higher characteristics of that planet to get to your North Node! It's a big deal; this is something you may have avoided doing in the past and needs to be looked at now.

Some of you *won't have any planets conjuncting either Node nor have a squared planet as a skipped step.* To get more information, *really follow the trail of the planet that rules your South Node and look at its sign, house and aspects as mentioned above.* This is important to do whether or not you have any aspects to your South Node—you must look at the planetary ruler of the South Node and follow its trail by house placement, sign and aspect.

And some of you may be looking at trines to your South Node and hoping for good news there— sorry! These trine planets may have encouraged lower South Node behavior—such as a friend dropping by with a bottle of wine after "forgetting" that you've gone sober. This could be a Venus trine the South Node; she's not helping a bit. Sometimes trines do have a supportive quality to them, but generally they have a lazy quality to them when it comes to Nodal analysis.

You can also read the planet opposing the South Node as not just representing a situation but more literally as a person who blocked or hurt you in the past. Moon in Scorpio opposing the South Node? Your mother could have been your biggest enemy to the path of your Soul. She may not have done it purposely but she may have demanded a behavior or a role that was totally wrong for you in that life. Or is Mercury there? Maybe it was a sibling that opposed you in that life. Play with the possibilities and also consider if there is still unfinished business with your current mother or sibling. We tend to get reborn into family groups where there remains unfinished karmic business.

ADDING THE CLUES: WHAT PLANET RULES YOUR SOUTH NODE SIGN? ARE THERE ANY PLANETS CONJUNCT IT?

*W*hat planet Rules your South Node Sign? (Rulers are listed here.) And, separately, are any of these planets or luminaries *conjunct* it? So, is the Sun, Moon or any of the planets conjunct your South Node? Add this piece to the puzzle.

Ruler of Leo: The Sun

If your Sun is the ruler or conjunct the SN you may have been in a position of power and there may have been too much Ego attachment in that life. You might also have had a heavy burden of responsibility on you, and your power may have resulted in loneliness. In this life you are called to be more open, call for less attention and to step outside of burdensome roles when necessary.

Ruler of Cancer: The Moon

If the Moon is the ruler or conjunct your SN there was deep involvement with the family, and chances are, since we read the SN negatively, that it was dysfunctionality that brought you pain. There could also have been something that went wrong with your past life parenting experience; a child could have had a mental illness, or died (is Pluto making aspects?) or was there alcoholism (is Neptune or Pisces involved?) or incest? (is Mars or Pluto also involved?)

You may have been defined by your family role, and certainly by the nurturing you received or the nurturing you didn't get. Emotional storminess in the past may have hindered your ability to think, so this time around you are called to bring in a balancing rational objective energy in all you do. (Donald Trump has this is a conjunction to his South Node.)

Ruler of Gemini and Virgo: Mercury

If Mercury is the ruler or conjunct your South Node your mind and your ability to communicate is highlighted, but since we read the SN as what you suffered from or didn't get quite right, you may have survived by fast talking that eclipsed your ability to tune into your heart and to think broadly.

If Saturn squares this Mercury you could even have been deaf. If not literally, you might have been a young person who didn't listen well, who reacted to events rather than thinking things through. If you suffered from that in the past, you know that communication skillfulness will be on the front burner in this life.

Ruler of Taurus and Libra: Venus

. . .

If Venus is the ruler or conjunct your South Node you are looking at relationship, gender and artistic complications. You could have been defined by your marriage relationship in an unhappy way (is the 7th house involved?) or with an abundance of Venusian characteristics you could have been an artist (any 5th house placements?) or you certainly could have been a female or a gay male who suffered from judgments in a former life (is Venus in Aquarius or in hard aspect to Uranus?) In this life you'll want to have Venus working for you, either through good discernment in relationships or thoughtful promotion of your artistic nature so you don't get caught in a kind of fame that leads to drug or alcohol issues or sexual escapism.

Ruler of Aries: Mars

If Mars is the ruler of, or conjunct your South Node, there could certainly have been a male incarnation before, and those problems connected with maleness, such as having to go to war or competition. If you were a warrior type you may have been rewarded for it as you defended the innocent—but you probably suffered from this as well.

We read the SN as that which we suffered from, and you could have killed the bad guy in any situation, and yet watched him die horribly in front of your eyes. Post traumatic syndrome for sure. You could have been nobly defending your family, but still the violence may have left its mark on your Soul. Now you come into this life with a residue of that pain, that anger, or fear. You may have a passion for justice now or for the deep healing this aspect calls for.

Ruler of Sagittarius: Jupiter

If Jupiter is the ruler or conjunct your South Node you may have been larger than life last time around. You likely were at least noticed and probably had some status and entitlement that came with your birth. There could have been pride—and yes, especially in this case, pride could come before a downfall! If the 5th house is involved with your Nodes, sexuality, children and creativity may have been misguided, or there could have been pomposity with connections to Saturn or Capricorn. The Moon and Cancer connections may suggest nurturing or food issues. In the 7th or 8th house you may have been the power behind the throne. But there was a downfall. You got caught in a soul cage: check out aspects to the rest of your Nodal story. Now in this life, over-confidence and pride need to be tempered. (Donald Trump has this as ruler of his South Node.)

Ruler of Capricorn: Saturn

If Saturn is the ruler of or conjunct your South Node there likely was considerable constriction and authoritarianism in your past life, and maybe huge responsibilities as well. You could have risen to them or collapsed under them. You may have lived in poverty raising six children. You had strength and integrity and did your best, but likely had no time or ability to open your heart and feel the sweetness of life. Moods were contained and restrained. There can be an underlying mood of depression with this conjunction, so part of the Soul purpose for you will be to heal in this life, and to regain your sense of joy.

. . .

Ruler of Aquarius: Uranus

If Uranus is the ruler of, or conjunct your SN, you carry the archetypes of either the outsider, the rebel or the exile within you. You were an independent person who danced to the beat of your own drummer, and who probably suffered much because of this. You also could have suffered from an unexpected shocking event such as a loss of position (is the 10th house or Capricorn involved?) or did you lose your money (2nd house or Taurus?) or your relationship (7th house involvement?) In this life you may feel an undertone of edgy anxiety but don't give in to social isolation—in fact—reach out to others and find ways to heal relationships. This time, there is love to be found.

Ruler of Pisces: Neptune

If Neptune is the ruler of or conjunct your SN you may have forgotten how to live. You could have succumbed to addictions in the past life or have given up something you really needed to live a full life! If it was food, there could be aspects to the

Moon or Cancer, or if it was sex there may be links to Venus, Mars or the 8th house. Fifth house links could indicate addictions. Sadly too, many religious beliefs in the past cut us off from our bodies and true spirituality, leading us to losing our higher sense of Self. You are called in this life to heal that dissociated person who you became; you are called to act out the higher resonance of Neptune which is a fuller sensitivity to all of life and a deep truer connection between your head and heart.

Ruler of Pluto: Scorpio

If Pluto is the ruler of or conjunct your South Node you may have been a victim or suffered from some sense of being in the "Underworld." You may have known horror and tragedy in a way most of us will never know. You could have been involved in a collective catastrophe such as a plague or war, or it could have been a personal catastrophe in which violence was involved. You could have been a victim or a victimizer, but either way you suffered from this descent into the Underworld. There's no reason for shame or blame now, but there's a huge call to healing with this aspect. Sometimes it takes lifetimes to get over tragedies, and also to understand the complexities of victims, rescuers and perpetrators. No one is immune to the dark side of life, but you may have unresolved issues that still need healing as a result of some kind of nightmare you lived through.

PLANETS OPPOSING YOUR
SOUTH NODE

*A*ny planet that is *opposing your South Node* is what you were up against in your past life, and it was something or someone that challenged and hurt you. The opposition means that you now have to understand and integrate those qualities and energies of the opposing planet in this life because you suffered from them before.

Any planet that is "square" (roughly ninety degrees) away from your South Node is in the position of being called *"the skipped step"* and it afflicted you in your last life. It may have done that then, and continues to do that now, especially if it's something you avoid. The skipped step is a part of yourself that you don't understand or act on. *A blind spot.* If it's in this square position you are meant to get to your North Node by means of that skipped planet. You can't avoid it; you are meant to "do" what that planet represents by sign and house in its highest octave.

Sun: If the Sun is opposing your South Node you were likely opposed in your soul journey by a powerful and authoritative "other" who pulled you into their orbit. Like being pulled by the Sun, you had to submit to its gravity. Your ego was diminished and you lost a certain capacity to be truly self-directed. You need a little bit of enlightened Selfishness in this life so that you can give yourself what you need, and build a strong ego and Self that will serve you well.

If this is your *skipped step*, concentrate on who and what you want to become in this lifetime. Make yourself a priority. It may look like career building or family building, but make sure it represents your heart and soul. Give it time to evolve.

. . .

Moon: If the Moon is opposing your South Node you probably came into this life with an emotional storminess about you. This could have been the result of your interaction with your Mother and secondarily your family. You may have been born with some dependency still on them along with an unexplained sense of resentment. They controlled you in your past life—as did your extreme moodiness. In this life you are called to nurture yourself deeply and to move away from too tight commitments to folks who may smother your individuality. You are meant to become your own person this time around.

When the Moon is square your Nodes and acting as a *skipped step*, you are called to notice your emotions and then to respond to them. Not just react. Accept the depth of your feelings but don't let them overwhelm you.

Mercury: If Mercury is opposing your South Node then in a prior life, or earlier in this one, you were out-shone by someone you perceived as being smarter than you. This could evolve into having doubts about your intelligence and a need to prove to yourself, and perhaps others, that you are indeed smart. Some of you might go the opposite direction for awhile and simply be an underachiever, but that's not great for you in the long run.

If Mercury is your *skipped step* then you truly need to "find your voice" in this life, and look to the sign and aspects to your Mercury to give you hints about how you think and what supports or challenges you. Either way, you are called not be become a person who is "always right" but rather to become a person who has a quiet self confidence in their own intellectual ability.

Venus: If you have Venus opposing your South Node, then you know that issues around relationship, gender and creativity were painful for you in your last life. Grace, creativity and art may have been blocked from you for some reason, and you likely yearned and suffered in relationships. You've come into this life with all that unresolved so you may feel incomplete without another person and you may pine for beauty, for elegance and the sweetness of life you missed out on. In this life you are called to make real-life Love work for you and to engage in the arts as much as it pleases you. Claim your voice and pick an honorable life partner.

If Venus is square to your SN and therefore your *skipped step* you'll want to look at the sign and placement of Venus to find out more. You are now called to go in the direction of this Venus, to integrate these qualities into yourself, and to go out of your way if necessary to learn how to be graceful and a person that others just want to love!

Mars: If you have Mars opposing your South Node, there was most likely some violence in your past. You could have been physically hurt, but also verbally abused in some ways. You came into this world with feeling of powerlessness, fear and perhaps rage, which you have to try to keep from erupting. You may now fear strength and anger and of even being seen. Now you are called to develop the traits of a spiritual warrior who has confidence in his or her own courage and power. You are called to be proud of yourself, and perhaps you've already done a lot of this empowering work in your life.

If Mars is square to your SN and therefore your *skipped step* you'll want to look at the sign and placement of Mars to find out more. But in a nutshell, you need to be capable of self defense whether it is verbally or physically. You don't need to fear others; instead only fear that you don't develop the self-empowerment that is calling to you.

Jupiter: If you have Jupiter opposing your South Node, then someone with status or personal authority may have opposed you. Or it may have been that you saw other people winning accolades and having charisma and abundance when you didn't. There could even be a left-over jealousy for those who claim the spotlight. In this life you are called to attain some kind of meaningful accomplishment and for you to be applauded for it. It may be risky, but having the idea of "I'm going for it!" is perfect for you in this life.

. . .

If Jupiter is square to your Nodes and therefore is your *skipped step* then you may be called to enlarge your life patterns, and to develop generosity of spirit. Dare to become as good as possible at what you do, and check the sign and house of this Jupiter as to clues. Obsession with people who have glamorous lives is a lazy way of living with this skipped step; don't do it—go for greatness yourself, even if in small ways.

Saturn: If you have Saturn opposing your South Node, then there's a good chance you have endured and suffered through hard times stoically, and often with self-sacrifice. You were dutiful; and probably depressed. Saturn makes for hard work and although there may have been some rewards for this in your past life, the mood that was carried over to this life wasn't cheerful. You served your family, or country and your God but perhaps forgot about your Self.

With Saturn square to the Nodes as *a skipped step*, you are called to taking the best Saturn has to offer; the chance to focus, concentrate and work hard.

And what does that get you? As different from the last life when Saturn opposed you, with it as your skipped step you're meant to do Saturn, and those who "do" Saturn are often rewarded. Doing Saturn is about paying your taxes as well as getting up at night to nurse the baby. It's also about bearing with the sometimes terrible things that happen to us in this life. We are called to endure a lot; but make an effort to keep it balanced with the small joys of life as well. Saturn rewards in the long run, although in the short run, it can feel like you're just taking out the garbage.

Uranus: If you have Uranus opposing your South Node, then you may have been struck by shock in a former life. You could have been abandoned as a child or attacked by someone "outside the law"— that's Uranus. Something was hard and sudden: perhaps you were standing under the volcano when it erupted, and you had no time to make your good-byes or reflect on your life. In this life now you may feel uneasy with people who are trouble-makers and those who live outside of the rules and laws. You may have some free floating anxiety about too sudden changes.

. . .

With Uranus in a square to your Nodes and as the *skipped step,* you are called to understand how to live by the spirit of the law but not always the letter of the law. That would be a challenge for you, but you need a little freedom. Uranus is about freedom and you need to find ways to bring freedom and change into your life. A good motto for you is: "Let's do something different." Check the sign and house placement to see where your cosmic permission slip is to color outside the lines.

Neptune: If you have Neptune opposing your South Node, then addiction and dependencies might have blurred your soul journey in a former life. You might also have allowed yourself to identify so strongly with a group, a person or a collective vision that you lost control of your common sense. Ungrounded beliefs and habits may have taken over. Conspiracy theories may have come in through the void by your weak ego—by your vacating your Self. You were so porous, perhaps due to misfortune or illness or lack of work that you allowed anything to come into your consciousness that gave meaning or even distraction. The facts? You didn't really care anymore; you may have been so worn down you simply needed to feel alive.

With Neptune as your *skipped step*, square to the Nodes, you are called to take up the higher octave of Neptune. That's usually seen as a sacred path; a path with heart. You don't lose yourself to another in this process but enter into right relationship with them and with what you believe. Neptune is fortunate when it is supported by a good relationship to the facts and to "Truth" and like good love affairs; there is discernment as well as chemistry involved. You are also wise if you feed yourself liberal doses of inspiration, for this feeds your Soul. I always imagine the glyph for Neptune as a little stick figure with its arms up to the heavens asking for inspiration. Find it—ask for it! Find ways to nourish yourself with the good and beautiful in your life.

Pluto: If you have Pluto opposing your South Node, then you have experienced a nightmare in a former life. You most likely came up against catastrophe or evil or victimization then and your primary task in this life is to heal from that experience.

You may have repressed memories or fears that are not grounded in this life—but they were in the previous one! You may not have been literally abused in this life, but somehow and in some unconscious way you know about it. You have experienced it. With this aspect you need to find the right kind of therapy that will ferret out the negative feelings—you don't need to remember the events— but simply to know that your feelings about catastrophes or criminals aren't just "all in your head." You've had some personal experience with the underside of life, and although you may have a confident attitude now, it may be jaded and rough edged unless you've done some healing work. You are meant to do more than just survive in this life. Goodness and even greatness is always part of the "gold" or riches of Pluto aspects.

If Pluto is square to your South Node, and is your *skipped step*, then you are meant to use Pluto to help you get over Plutonian nightmares. That is, like a homeopathic remedy where the cure/remedy is found in the disease itself you are called to do some deep work in this life. On your Soul passport, you have the stamp of Pluto: "Been there, done that." You now are savvy enough that you can help others; it could be in law-enforcement, or as a therapist or many others things where you benefit from knowing how the other person thinks and feels. For you too, just healing itself is a major victory and when you look at the sign and house placement of this skipped step in your chart you'll know where to look "under the covers" of mundane respectability to find what's really going on.

SOME SPECIAL CONSIDERATIONS

*W*hat *if the Ruler of your North or South Node is conjunct the opposite Node?* This means that the road forward in your life really involves your past: re-living, re-experiencing the personal pain you've lived through and gaining personal insights from this process. It's really a call to psychotherapy. You can heal yourself best by truly going deep to understand the roots of your pain.

Reversed Nodes in Signs and Houses: And what if you have a confusing situation with the Nodes and Houses? The signs and houses are in their opposite places?

Again, this is when you have to clearly separate the meaning of the houses from the meaning of the signs. They are not the same, although it may appear to be so at first glance. The houses describe where the action is happening. "Where" is the key word. The Sign describes what is happening, what we're exploring here, but not where it's happening in your life.

An example (because I know this is a hard question for many readers): what if you have the North Node in Aries but it's in the 7th house? And that would put your South Node in Libra in the 1st house?

So in that example, you might say: With the NN in Aries in the 7th house you are meant to hold your own identity, your own courage and feistiness and independence in the area of marriage and partnerships (7th house), because in a past life you may have done your SN Libra (in the first house) as total enmeshment with a partner, and lost yourself.

And lastly, what if the Ruler of your South Node is your skipped step? This hints that you were your own worst enemy in a former life...and even now! You afflicted yourself, and you may repeat that pattern again unless you meditate on the meaning of that planet and sign that is the skipped step. If your SN ruler was Pluto, and you have Pluto squaring it, then you might have been your own worst enemy. What might have happened to lead your there? What behavior did you repeat over and over again and just not get it right?

And when you start looking at your Nodal story from your "Past Life" you may say: but that's just what happened *in the first part of this life*! This is actually what usually happens, *you repeat the past until you have the insight to stop that behavior and begin anew*. This can happen at any stage of your life, but often starts to happen around the age of the first Saturn Return at 29 years. However, *the Nodes are something we work on our whole life*. You may find that at your Second Saturn Return you are called to revisit them again to see how to best go into the next stage of your life.

The South Node is more formally called "the South Node of the Moon"—so how is it related to my Moon?

Here's a good question a reader asked in my blog on

the South Node: *"Why were you writing yesterday about the South Node and the Moon together?"* And I replied: I'm doing this because they mutually reinforce each other and tell more of the story of the heart.

Yes, they each are different—in that the Moon describes your emotional and nurturing style in this life and how you relate to all things "maternal" including your Mother. However, the Moon's Nodes are about the "unconscious emotional memory" that can often relate to issues around being nurtured or the lack of it.

And because the South Node specifically holds the *emotional memory* of the Soul, the story goes back further in time. It speaks of the emotional memory (not linear or left-brain memory) that is carried over from life to life. I believe this memory is sometimes called "skandas" in Hinduism, or you could think of it as something embedded in your DNA.

I find that the overlapping and synthesizing of the two is fascinating...have you considered how your Moon sign and South Node sign reflect something of your conscious and unconscious patterns related to issues around nurturing? It's a possibility worth considering. As is the chapter I wrote on the"family karmic inheritance" in my book *North Node Astrology*. Family emotional traits, including "nurturing" styles, get handed down the family line through generations, and we may see some of that karmic inheritance reverberating in the Moon, the Moon's Nodes, and 12th house planets.

Let's say your South Node is in Scorpio, ruled by Pluto, and your Moon is in Aries ruled by Mars. The ancient story embedded in your psyche may be deeply Plutonian, powerful, and perhaps tragic. And so, in this life your Soul chose to be born with a Mars ruled Aries Moon-- maybe your Soul knew in some mysterious way that now you needed to "survive, to have courage, to start fresh, and to be enthusiastic" rather than brooding; sounds like a description of a life affirming Aries Moon to me. Maybe that Aries Moon person is somewhat irritable, impulsive, and independent--it might just be that the South Node in Pluto ruled Scorpio reflected a heavy karmic *maternal* inheritance. And perhaps to survive it, independence and courage was needed.

So, it's similar to when Sun sign astrologers say: look at your Rising Sign as well as your Sun sign in reading about yourself because each has a message here--and I would add, that when you are looking at your South Node sign, look at your Moon as well. What secrets or subtleties are there? Read both.

"THE CHART BENEATH THE CHART"

*a*s fellow astrologer Caroline Casey so accurately once said in a radio show:

"Astrology represents a voice of the irrational, mystical, spirit domain which says that everything is interconnected and interrelated and that you can't pluck one strand of creation without resonating it all. It corresponds to a very real hunger people have for mystery, for things are mysteriously connected. Astrology says that cynicism is just intellectual laziness. There's no future in nihilism; one has to believe and have faith in something; a larger process."

· · ·

I love that feisty statement, because it speaks to the mysterious spirit domain that underlies astrology and particularly this kind of astrology where we are attempting to read "the chart beneath the chart." As said in the beginning of the book we always look first at the traditional triad of Sun, Moon and Rising Sign and then we add on the Nodes. This is reaching for the deeper mystery; the chart beneath the chart.

EXAMPLES: Let's look at *Donald Trump's chart* for a moment. Here we see a man with a Gemini Sun in the 10th house of public image conjunct the North Node and the rebellious planet, Uranus. The South Node is in Sagittarius, conjuncting the Moon. Rising sign is Leo, with Mars on the Ascendant.

Here's a typical interpretation of the triad of Sun, Moon and Rising:

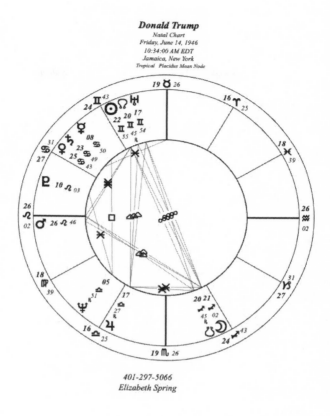

Donald Trump
Natal Chart
Friday, June 14, 1946
10:34:00 AM EDT
Jamaica, New York
Tropical Placidus Mean Node

401-297-5066
Elizabeth Spring

Gemini Sun: As an air sign you are inclined towards the world of ideas and conversational debate. Always curious, you have a wide range of interests and dislike being bored. Playful and mischievous, you can at times, be superficial and inclined to flit from one thing to another.

Sagittarius Moon: As a fire sign you have a natural enthusiasm and ambition. Freedom is essential for you to follow your natural tendency to see life as a "Quest." You tend to be optimistic, expansive, philosophical. Sagittarius is known as the salesman, the storyteller, and the exaggerator of the astrological world. There's often a funny and kind side to you, although the lower octave of expression tends to be indulgent and judgmental. There can be a tendency to brag or to place oneself as judge.

Leo Rising: Your primary motivation is to attain power and recognition. You make an impact on others through displaying a commanding personality. Self-confident, you carry yourself with dignity. You like being the center of attention and being a leader and organizer. You tend to have a sensitive ego and a lot of pride; arrogance and stubbornness can turn others against you.

. . .

We can add on to that basic information by noting the planets opposite the South Node and conjunct the North Node; Uranus and the Sun. Here we can see a man who is clever and fast talking (Gemini) with Uranus, the planet that acts unconventionally and rules the internet, conjuncting the North Node in the 10th house of career and public image. We can see the maverick and rebellious nature of Uranus here in that he refused to accept the consensus judgment of his election results, and that he didn't communicate with his people in the usual Presidential ways, but instead used Twitter to spit out phrases like "crooked Hilary" and "Sleepy Joe" and "Go back to where you came from."

With Trump's Sun conjuncting his North Node, one could rightly say he was destined to be a man of note and stature. One could also say that he felt up against the Father and Authority in a former life— the Sun—and in this one too. One way to handle this is not to rebel but to become what one is up against. We see that he became like his father and followed his father's authority.

· · ·

His South Node conjuncting the Moon, implies a past life where emotional lunar expression would be an important part of his life. Now one looks at his early family history and wonders if his emotional nurturing needs weren't being met? He was up against a powerful authority figure in his father; his father represented here by the Sun opposing him. What else is opposing him? Uranus; the outlaws, the outsiders. We can see that he turned to *becoming what he was up against: Uranus.* Perhaps he turned to it to make it work for him as the outlaws/outsiders/Proud Boys and angry white men? Indeed. Uranus is conjunct the North Node so he would be called to use rebelious Uranus in some capacity. (The storming of the Capital?) He also used his Solar personality and father (the Sun) to further him on in his life and career.

With Uranus here on the Nodal axis, it would be imperative that he take the high road, and use the innovative and unpredictable Uranus to bring his Soul Journey into alignment. Uranus is also the planet of the "Rebel" and the fringe elements in society, and he had a problem with being presidential and diplomatic: with his South Node and Moon in the notorious "Foot in Mouth" sign of Sagittarius, he suffered from verbal outbursts that sounded more like bullying and name calling. He probably didn't mean for some of his impassioned statements to be interpreted the way they were, but what happens if we follow the trail of his ruling planet of his North Node, Sun and Uranus? Mercury, his planet of communication— is *square to the confusing and illusion prone planet Neptune,* so it's not surprising that there was so much controversy over true facts and false statements, true news and fake news.

And what happens if we follow the trail of the ruler, Jupiter, of his South Node Sagittarius? Jupiter is in the second house which rules money. It has a trine to Uranus symbolizing an almost magical ability to manifest whatever he wants, although from an esoteric perspective, magical power that is directed by the ego instead of the higher self can result in one's undoing rather than success. And if there is a lower octave of any sign in the zodiac that might suggest his larger-than-life persona and his style of bullying, on the internet and otherwise, it might very well be *Jupiter ruled Sagittarius. Sign of his*

South Node. As we know he was raised in a military boys school and that he succumbed to patterns of bullying there, and most likely a misogynistic view of women was born there as well. Pornography is as common as pimples at boys school, but it leaves a worse scar. The Mother/Whore complex is often born in these situations as are issues around one's masculinity and sexuality. What emerged for Donald Trump is a person who could lead a life where the women were either the mistress (remember "Stormy Daniels") or the mother-wife who kept quiet most of the time: (Melania.)

It appears that Trump's blustery nature hid a more sensitive and wounded soul. He has 3 planets in Cancer. Cancer wants to nurture and care for, like a mother caring for her young. I believe Trump genuinely believed that he knew what was best for us.

And look again at his South Node conjuncting his Moon in the 4th house: family, tradition, mother and real estate, all ruled by the controlling hand of Scorpio on the cusp of 4th house. Here we see family focus; and perhaps some mother issues in that Moon. If we look at the South Node opposing the Sun, often representing the father, we get a hint of authority and father issues.

The Sun, ruling the father and Moon ruling the mother, oppose each other just like the Nodes. The ruler of his South Node Sagittarius is Jupiter, and Jupiter squares Saturn (father, fear, restriction). The ruler of his North Node is Mercury, and Mercury is in Cancer; sign of the mother and emotions. Mercury is square to Neptune suggesting confusion in speech and the Cancerian quality hints of the pressure of the family karmic legacy.

Where do we look for some of the secrets of the chart, as well as the family karmic inheritance? In the 12th house of the deep psyche and unconscious he has Pluto: Lord of the Underworld and hidden riches. What is hidden away? Could it be finances? Or something else connected with the Underworld? And with Mars in Leo on the Leo Ascendant—here is a blustery Kingly drive—that could stand as a guard to keep anyone away from his vulnerability.

· · ·

In a former life, and as a hidden aspect in this life, we could see a person who needed love, a heart, and true courage. Not only does his Venus conjuncting Saturn hint at the possibility of having unmet emotional/relational needs, but the Moon is conjunct his South Node and ruler of those Cancer planets. Here is a person, with an orange tinted complexion and wild mane, like the Cowardly Lion in the Wizard of Oz who needed courage; who needed validation. He needed to receive a "heart" and so he did, receiving the Purple Heart from a Veteran. But what act of courage was this for?

The Nodes in this chart underscore what we see in the reading of the traditional birth chart, but the "chart beneath the chart" underlines the importance of Trump taking the high road if he was called to be a person of destiny—not the South Node gold gilded Jupiterian road that would make him feel entitled; entitled to dismiss or bully or incite to riot. (Interesting how the main color scheme in his house is gold.)

With that Gemini North Node he was called to be a

bridge builder, not a divisive leader. He could have been a person who used his Mercurial Gemini knowledge of the "marketplace" to help the common man and to unite all people. But when we follow the trail of Mercury and we see it squaring Neptune which kept him out of touch with the world of reality we see a problem. With Mercury, good clear communication is key and we see that he didn't have that in his life, nor did he have it as President.

And remember how his Nodes are conjunct his Sun and Moon—perhaps the most important points in his chart. He needed to heal his South Node conjunct the Moon family karmic inheritance. He needed to monitor his Sagittarius over-doing and foot in mouth disease and use that Uranus energy in a tenth house fashion: with Capricorn-like decorum and integrity. If he were to succumb to the lower octave of his Nodes in Sagittarius and Gemini he might speak and live "Loud" (Jupiter and Mercury)—and although he might be charismatic on the public stage of the 10th house, he might have failed his life lessons. Or he might simply have done his best this time around. (For more look again at the South Node Sagittarius chapter.)

Let's look at an entirely different kind of chart, that of *Edna St.Vincent Mill*ay who was a much-loved American poet, known for her poignant love poetry, and for her eccentric life of free love and glamour.

Born in 1892 she became one of the world's most famous women poets; although she is now seen as old-fashioned in style—

"Whose lips my lips have kissed

and where and why,

I have forgotten,

and what arms have lain

under my head till morning;

but the rain is full of ghosts tonight,

that tap and sigh upon the glass and listen for reply,
and in my heart there stirs a quiet pain for
unremembered lads that not again

will turn to me at midnight with a cry.

Thus in the winter stands the lonely tree, nor knows
what birds have vanished one by one,

Yet knows its boughs more silent than before:

I cannot say what loves have come and gone,

I only know that summer sang in me a little while,
that in me sings no more."

Powerful and poignant! Yet this is not the kind of
poetry that is subtle and complex enough for most
literary magazines today. But she was the most
well-loved poet of her generation, also writing
heroic poems for encouragement of the American
troops during W.W.II. She was the Amanda Gorman
of her age, having the petite charisma and charm of
a stunning young woman.

Edna ST. Vincent Millay
Natal Chart
Monday, February 22, 1892
6:05:00 AM EST
Rockland, Maine
Tropical Placidus Mean Node

401-297-5066
Elizabeth Spring

Edna, known as "Vincent" was born with a Pisces
Sun, Moon in Sagittarius, and Aquarius rising. The
South Node was in Scorpio, in the 9ᵗʰ house, and
the North Node in Taurus Third house. She also had
a Pluto/Neptune conjunction in that 3ʳᵈ house that

squared her Sun. Mercury, the planet of communication, was on her Ascendent and squaring her Nodes. Her 10th house of public image was occupied by Mars conjuncting her Moon in the sign of Sagittarius.

Vincent truly lived her birth chart and hypnotized and inspired readers—one could say she made of her poems an erotic autobiography. A graduate of Vassar, she wrote poems of heterosexual, lesbian, and free love. Yet she suffered from pain and illnesses all her life—finally leading up to severe addictions to drugs and alcohol.

A reading of her chart in the traditional manner, shows a person unconventional (Aquarius Rising) inspired and larger than life (Pisces Sun and Jupiter first house) with a passionate nature (Mars conjunct the Moon.) If she was our client, we would warn her of dangers due to poisons with Pluto conjunct Neptune squaring her Sun, and indeed she struggled with drinking and drug use all her life, finally dying tragically of alcoholism.

·   ·   ·

When we look at her Nodes we see a Soul that has come into this world with a background of Plutonian trauma and drama (South Node Scorpio ruled by Pluto) who would have been wise to seek serenity in this life (North Node Taurus). We see Pluto at the base of her chart, the Nadir, conjunct Neptune, the planet that rules poisons among other things. Her North Node in the 3rd house would have favored her life as a writer (as would the Mercury on Ascendent) and her South Node in the 9th might suggest she had experienced other cultures and learning, and had developed a self-convincing story of how life was put together. In this life she would need the experience of the market-place of life to live her journey. She could not be isolated like Emily Dickenson, because of her North Node in the 3rd house.

Her North Node in Taurus is ruled by Venus and we see Venus in her first house in Aries. She lived up to this Aries by being a pioneer in her time—a graduate of Vassar, and a well-loved and respected writer. She took risks and dared to be all she could be. At only five feet tall she was an imposing and strong character who dared to travel the world, raise thorough-bred horses, and be with almost any man or woman she wanted.

Men and women were in awe of her erotic Venusian nature, but not of the lower octave of her Aries Venus, wild and uncompromising, that took away from her the sweet calm nature that Venus so often can have…for Vincent, life became one of extremes and led to an early death, poisoned by her love of ecstatic states. Venus took her too far; and ultimately to her death.

There are no planets conjuncting the Nodes, but Mercury at 22 degrees Aquarius squares them—this is the skipped step. She is called in this life to write, to be a communicator and a bridge builder. She would have suffered from an inability to do this in a former life, being constrained with Mercury in some way—yet now she is called to take up this "skipped step" and to express her life. In this she radically succeeded.

But what is the ruler of the South Node doing? In

her case it is Pluto and we see Pluto conjoining with Neptune; the poison I spoke of earlier. She died of alcoholism. The higher octave of Pluto would be to go to the depths of emotions in her writing and to the transcendent heights of Neptune—which she did in her poetry and in her search for ecstatic Dionysian union in love. However, these planets which hover near the base of her chart—the Nadir —hold a great potential for pain and suffering. In their lower modes of expression, Pluto rules that which can kill us in the Underworld and Neptune rules the confused and altered realities we can sink into—and that was indeed her nemesis and her tragic death due to a misuse of "Spiritus." An evolutionary astrologer might have suggested something that Carl Jung and Bill W. often told their clients: that only "Spiritus Contra Spritus" (Only Spirit can counteract the effects of spirits.)

FOLLOWING THE NODES: MY STORY

*L*et's *look at an example of this spiritual detective story from my chart.*

Here we'll follow the trail of South Node in Scorpio in the 8th house, conjunct Jupiter, to the North Node in Taurus 2nd house. The ruler of the South Node Pluto is in a wide orb skipped step to Pluto and Saturn in the 5th house. The chart holds a lot of "I— Thou" tension in the balance of the Libra stellium in the 7th house with the Aries Rising and Aries Moon. The T-square to Mars in Leo is softened by its trine to Jupiter and the South Node, but trines to the Nodes are not seen as a major mitigating force in Evolutionary Astrology. They suggest some support and sympathy but not a major theme. The Sun-

Neptune conjunction is challenging and also supportive as is the Uranus trine Mercury, and Pluto trine the Ascendant.

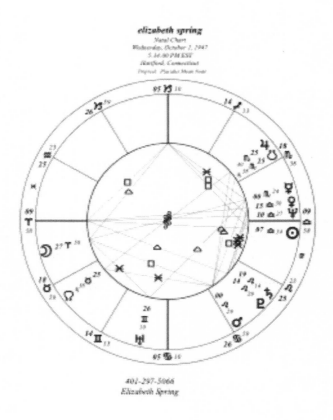

Here is a South Node in Scorpio, ruled by Pluto, in the 8th house, with the North Node in Taurus, ruled by Venus, in the 2nd house. There's a wide 90

degree angle –a skipped step--to Saturn and Pluto in the 5th house. The Sun is in a stellium in Libra with Aries Rising and Aries Moon. How does the story go?

I grew up at a time (the 1950's) in a family where there was a quiet atmosphere of unspoken anger and the occasional eruptions of drama, along with a whiff of Jupiterian entitlement. There was a Germanic or Plutonian kind of unspoken strictness and darkness in my home that I didn't understand. My parents loved their little daughter but although I was encouraged to succeed I realized they didn't respect women in the world who achieved anything because of their intellects or work ethic. Eleanor Roosevelt was frowned upon, and Marilyn Monroe was approved of; women were sexual sweeties or wives who should stay home bound. I lived in an early childhood Plutonian atmosphere that affronted my very human nature and I developed an unconscious smoldering anger at the misogyny that permeated my world. As soon as I finished high school I left home, despite keeping relatively close personal ties to my parents. But I couldn't exist in such an atmosphere.

I see most of the repetition of my Nodes happening

for me in my childhood, teens and twenties. It was during the teen years and early twenties that I made decisions in love affairs that were often heart-breaking and disillusioning. It was only until around the age of thirty at my first Saturn Return that I began to integrate the gifts of my North Node Taurus. But each Node is an inseparable part of the other; for good and not so good.

In my late teens, with a South Node in Scorpio I begin getting caught up in other people's lives and values. I was a child of the sixties and allowed myself to get seduced into the lives of others (8th house) who were primarily musicians with larger than life personalities (Jupiter conjunct South Node.) The 8th house tendency to overly concern or to lose oneself in other's values was reinforced by its Scorpio placement—and yes, it was a lot of sex, drugs and rock & roll—in my case mostly folk music, but the dynamic was the same.

The ruler of Scorpio is Pluto, and Pluto/Saturn was also my skipped step in my 5th house of pleasure, creativity and love affairs. In some ways I've repeated some of my past life story in this life. I think we all do. I don't want to shout that out in this book, but I hope readers can see that in their lives;

that we keep repeating the same old story. It's not easy to change until we see the pattern.

In my chart, it's notable that the "skipped step" going to the authoritarian Saturn/ Pluto conjunction in the 5th house, suggested that there was some stern and cool reactions to whatever I did. I l believe I've suffered from that in both lives. I'm sure I repeated many of the same behaviors in both lives; the same reactionary impulse. Hopefully I take responsibility for the good and not-so-good.

The skipped step for me lies in the 5th house which rules creativity, children, love affairs and seeking joy. I call this 5th house the house that Joseph Campbell "built" because of the idea he promoted of following one's own "bliss" and in this house is Mars, Saturn and Pluto in Leo. Not easy blissful planets! On the positive side, having a child was one of the most challenging and rewarding things I have done. Writing books has been a huge amount of work; and pleasure. Times of "fun" usually have to be scheduled into my life (Saturn in 5th.)

My South Node enhanced the drama of my younger years, and although I had a certain status or largeness (Jupiter) in this small musical world I was the silent one. My sense of Self was weak (Neptune conjunct Sun.) Having been raised with a family background that had only minor expectations for me as a girl, I nevertheless did manage to follow a course of study through life--that although duplicitous in many ways--led me along a safer road than many people with patterns such as this have taken. When I think of how many children of the 60's died because of drug issues, I'd have to say that there was perhaps a little luck in my Jupiter conjunction.

As I followed my Nodal journey unknowingly, I longed for my own talents to come out and to be self-sufficient. My North Node in Taurus in the 2nd house was pulling me to be grounded and to live by my own resources. I had no other planets in Earth other than my North Node. For so many years I had been living in a dream world (Sun conjunct Neptune and Venus) and with Pluto as Ruler of Scorpio and the 8th house— squaring my Nodes—well, Pluto aspects like this can send you to hell and back. My heart was constantly being broken by others and by myself, as I lived a roller-coaster life between illusory heavens and hells. The loneliness was intense.

Intuitively. and with gathering courage (Aries Moon) I summoned the psychic resources necessary to move across country, go to graduate school and to begin to be self-sufficient as a potter. There were many death/rebirth Pluto/Scorpio scenarios in those years and the gift of Pluto/Scorpio is regeneration. I was able to tap into that.

My Venus ruled Taurus North Node drew me to making pottery at that time and I created a series of small shops and began studying astrology more earnestly. I began depending less on others and more on myself—eventually marrying a Virgo potter--my Venus is in the 7th house of marriage.

I also had a significant Near Death Experience in my early twenties and was told by "God" or my Higher Self, that I desperately needed to ground myself in this world...same as my North Node message. The clay work, the making of my own money, and marrying a Virgo man with a lot of Earth in his chart all helped.

In the middle of my life, the pottery and focus on family life with a very sweet daughter, was fulfilling and eventually evolved into a life as a full-time astrologer and writer as well. In my forties I decided to go back to graduate school and get a Master's Degree in counseling psychology, with an emphasis in the work of Carl Jung. My astrology and writing have evolved into being my true work and gift to the world.

However, there is an *invisibility* in my Pluto ruled South Node; in mythology Pluto wears a helmet that makes him invisible. And I too, despite having achieved success in my work life as an astrologer and author (this is my 6th book) I've noticed that even "friends" don't know who I am. A part of me remains held in the invisible hold of the South Node Pluto/Scorpio. So many people I know and love have seldom read my books, nor heard my podcast, nor care to know my story. Astrology has a limited appeal. Whereas strangers, clients and others support my life and work. Perhaps the fact that I've been drawn towards the "occult" world of astrology and Theosophy have blinded the eyes of many who I wish would have cared to know me more. My parents never knew me; I don't remember them even seeing me throw a pot on the wheel and they refused to listen to any astrological reference. Although we loved each other, the dynamic for their generation and for my particular chart was unyielding. I didn't try to change them and they didn't try to change me; I just separated from them. The areas of the heart where we loved each are still there, it's just not the whole story. Family secrets were also a big part of my parents generation and secrets tend to fester within families. We owe each other the truth.

But the pull of my North Star, the North Node in Taurus in the 2nd house, helped ground me and made me prove myself to be worthy. Yet the heaviness of the Pluto/8th house still isolates, and yet it's one of the sources of my ability to be empathic doing astrological consults (been to Pluto and back!) and to draw from a source of wisdom outside my own. The Taurus North Node is a life saver, but perhaps not a Soul saver. We embody both our past and future and few people really know who we really are. I'm not alone. I do believe if I can understand my past life story more completely, and if others can do the same, we'll be opening up a portal of wisdom and compassion for us all. This book is part of my effort to understand more deeply.

The trail of Pluto from being the ruler of the 8th house Scorpio South Node, to being the skipped step with Saturn in the 5th house in Leo, enables me to understand the need to heal from trauma and drama inherent there, and reach for the peace of 2nd house North Node in Taurus. I believe I have regained a sense of Self that I lost in a former life as well as early in this one.

This is a hint of the story of how I played out my Nodes in this life so far. What about the past life story? What had I failed at, and what did I need to learn? One has to think of this as a parable, or a myth, not a literal truth, but with my Taurus/Second house North Node, it appears I was called to self-sufficiency: emotionally, physically, spiritually and financially. When I think of a parable of a past life with a South Node Scorpio and its Plutonian nature, with Jupiter there as well, I could see myself as being the invisible "power behind the throne" to someone of some status, and I could have strayed into a painful love affair (fifth house) with someone else (a traveling musician perhaps who was wandering through? ~grin~)

With that Pluto/Saturn being in the 5th house of love affairs and squaring the Nodes, I do believe I suffered from my actions: I may have had a child from that affair and been banished—and there would have been hard Saturnian consequences with

Saturn being conjunct Pluto. There would have been high drama and serious repercussions.

And in this life, with all the Leo in my 5th house, I have physical heart problems that may be a literal metaphor for the past pain. The deep meaning of the 5th house of creativity, children and love relationships is about joy. I get great joy from my daughter, my husband and my creativity. I believe I was meant to recover this sense of joy as well as a Taurus sense of serenity in this life.

THE NODAL RETURNS AND
TRANSITS TO YOUR NODES

The Nodal Returns happen at ages 18, 37, 55, 74, and 92. The Nodes take roughly 18.6 years to travel around the chart, and when they come back to their original spot—when your transiting North Node conjoins up again with your natal North Node—then you have a "Return." And automatically the transiting South Node will be on your natal South Node. This Return of the Nodes is a significant time in the same way that the Saturn "Returns" are significant at ages 29 and 59.

The Nodes are often called the "Points of Destiny" so they shouldn't be dismissed because they're not a planetary body. In fact, they are important in terms of fate, destiny, and awareness. At *roughly* these ages: 18, 37, 55, 74 and 92, the karmic wave may be breaking for you. It can be a turning point.

At these points you may have a date with destiny. You may have a fated meeting with someone who changes your life, or you may have a powerful personal epiphany that puts the pieces of your life together. It could be a positive or negative experience, but either way you have turned the wheel in your evolutionary life to a marking spot. If it is a negative experience it may be a repeat of a past life habit that you've lived through again, but this time you learn your lesson. Try for a moment and think over these ages; can you remember something significant happening at any of these times?

For me, my experience was simple but memorable. I was listening to music in a circle with a group of friends and daydreaming. Then I looked down at my open hands and saw—and felt—that I was having a *rebirth*. I was conscious of my Soul in a way I've never experienced before, and it felt as if my conscious and unconscious selves were coming together. My left hand clasped and joined with my right hand and they agreed to work in tandem. There was an awareness that a new part of me was being born. Nothing special. But in retrospect I remember this being just short of my 19 birthday and although nothing of worldly significance happened I never forgot this moment in time.

It may be that you begin to move in the direction indicated by your natal North Node Placement. You feel like you're going somewhere and there may be a strengthening and a clarity. Or you learn from experience what to do or not to do. For me, I began pottery classes and began to have an interest in astrology while I was at Boston University. Perhaps most important was that I saw honored myself in a way I had never done before. I'm sure it helped too that I was in love for the first time.

What about the "Inverse" Return; the Nodal Opposition?

. . .

This happens at roughly ages 8, 27, 45, 64 and 82. Some say this is "when your future meets your past." It can be a time when you've finally gained closure on past events so that now you're freer to move forward in your life. Or it may be a feeling that everything is turned upside down in order to give you a different perspective. You might come out of denial now, and turn past vulnerabilities and shame into self-worth. Or it could be a wake-up call. For me, at age 64 I wrote a memoir/novel called: *Saturn Returns; The Private Papers of a Reluctant Astrologer.*

What about a planetary transit over the Nodes? Or the Nodes transiting over a planet?

The kaleidoscopic effect of a planetary transit over the Nodes could be thought of as a specific re-alignment with the evolutionary needs of the Soul, having to do with the nature of that planet. Is it a transit of Mars, calling for more assertiveness? Or a transit of Saturn calling for more focus and concentration?

And, it's good to keep remembering how the Nodes are a polarity—that when one Node is transited by a planet, it reverberates its polar opposite as well. A transiting planet over a Node is read the same way as any transiting planet is read, except that on the Nodal axis we are hitting a harmonic chord about "life direction and soul purpose" (North Node) and "past life karma" (South Node.) It may be a subtle shift rather than one "event" in the world, but as we know, we're not in control with how a transit will play out in our lives.

Most of us would like to feel that we do have control over our life, and we surely have some control by the choices we make and how much consciousness and intention we bring to them. We have control over our response to transits, but because so much of the psyche operates from a base of unconsciousness, there's a mystery as to how and why things play themselves out the way they do. Perhaps that's another reason why we need to be gentle with ourselves. What's good for the ego, is not always good for the soul evolution.

. . .

So when a planet transits our Nodes, or our Nodes transit a planet, this may be an evolutionary re-alignment and we see now for a little while through the lens of the planet that is aspected or aspecting. For example, a transit of Jupiter to our Nodal axis may bring us into surprise contact with a mentor or supporter, and with a transit of Pluto we might find ourselves in psychotherapy or exploring "regression therapy." Always, it's not about good or bad, despite how it feels. Emotional lunar feelings change so fast and are unreliable in judging the long term effect of what the evolutionary intent is— again we must be gentle with the "universe" as well as ourselves.

IS THE LIFE YOU ARE LIVING TOO SMALL FOR YOU?

*C*hances are the answer to that question is some variation of yes. Chances are, the question may arouse some anxiety because that thought poses a variety of challenges, some big and some small. It hints of change and it's not exciting to think that a "larger life" could mean the disruption or potential loss of the goodness that you have in your life right now. But it doesn't have to be that way.

Let me share an example from my life. Towards the end of my Second Saturn Return at age fifty-nine, I remember sitting on my porch thinking that "Nothing is happening!" Astrologically I knew this was supposed to be a time of change, and nothing was remarkable. I thought, perhaps I need to take the initiative and take a class, or something even larger, so I signed up for a years apprenticeship in astrology. (Saturn loves "work!")

Long story short, at the end of the apprenticeship I was so inspired I wrote my first book, and then throughout my sixties I wrote five books altogether. Now in my seventies this is my sixth book. The point of this is that it was only in retrospect that I saw how that Saturn Return was a major turning point. A life-changing shift from being a counselor to a writer as well. There's plenty of life after sixty! However, it wasn't without its problems because I also overdid it with my writing, and at times caused too much stress. That ended up with me having some heart problems; but they were manageable. Hopefully you can make your changes more smoothly.

It is exciting to think there may be ways we might "recreate our self" and our lives to move towards a larger life without chaos or loss. Some writers have suggested that it is mostly a weakness in the muscle of our imagination that keeps us from being and doing all we could be. There are other very practical reasons why we don't or can't do certain things we'd like to do. I'm sure you're reminding yourself of those things now as you read this.

But consider this. It's true that change and re-creation are easier said than done. Here's an analogy—if we think of the astrology chart as a committee meeting of all the "planetary voices" in your psyche—all sitting around a conference table with the aspect lines in the center as the lines of communication between these voices—then you, as moderator of this committee, can tell certain parts of yourself to be quiet and others to speak up.

If we think of these planetary archetypes as members of our inner committee that are asking to be "listened to" then we can open up to new possibilities from those parts of our self that have been silenced...or at least those parts of our self that have been made to sit quietly with hands folded. As chairperson of this committee, you can listen to those members that know how to find ways to increase your capacity for joy and energy.

It is also true that sometimes you simply have to wait till the time is right. When the planetary voices in our psyche are stimulated by strong transits—that is, when other "committee members" come to their aid by conjunction or trine they get stronger. Even when strong planetary transits make hard aspects to these lesser heard "committee members" within us, we have a unique opportunity to give them a voice.

Life has a way of forcing us back into old patterns and listening to the old voices that have spoken the loudest before—and so we listen again to the same "loud-mouths" and wounded parts of our psyche and tend to repeat the same old solutions to the same old story. Yes, we know that crazy, but we too often get a little lazy until life gets uncomfortable enough to encourage change. Then we become better listeners.

So now you may be wondering if wounded Saturn and ruthless Pluto have talked enough? Maybe you're getting tired of reacting to the default patterns of your South Node? What about the gifts of Jupiter and the healing medicine in your North Node? Have you allowed Uranus to stop acting like an adolescent rebel and let him really loose? What would his version of freedom and inventiveness really look like?

The family karmic inheritance enters in here as well. Have you been blocked by fear, unconscious anxiety, or resistance to change because you're allowing ancient family patterns to repeat themselves in your life now? Do you really want to live in reaction or in repetition of your father? Or mother?

Have you thought of where you avoid conflict and thereby avoid the necessary conflict of values that allows you to be true to yourself? Is your Venus always going along with things? Or is she so scared she's trying to control the show and still not happy? Is your Moon sadly looking for permission or guidance from someone who may never show up? Is your Neptune demanding unconditional love or squirming with passive-aggressive confusion?

Interesting questions. Call for a committee meeting. Now may very well be the time to answer the summons of your Soul and to reach for your largest life. Isn't it time to call for a life review with you as moderator and recording secretary? You could take notes. Read old journals. You could write a 12 page autobiography. (I did that at each of my Saturn Returns and I recommend that to all my clients.) You could let all the planetary archetypes in your chart get a chance to speak. You could research some of the ideas you've had in the past and some of the ideas that may have been thrown out then may now be workable if you change the story script of your life. How you see your life narrative changes. Why not truly consider some "deep listening" at this time?

"LET GO OF YOUR DISTRACTIONS BEFORE THEY ROB YOU OF YOUR LIFE."

The South Node holds your distractions, your old habits, and your reactive tendencies—all those things that rob you of your authentic life. It's familiar and easy to "frame" the story of your life in terms of your old life, because you know it—life has showed you certain things up until now, so that this is your reality. It doesn't have to be that way. The negative qualities of the South Node have shown you where you've been and what you're bringing over from a past life or from earlier in this one. It reflects your family karmic inheritance, and your particular karmic story. It's old, it's tired, it's familiar—and it's not the whole story!

The North Node is what the Soul aspires to, and by following the positive qualities of its sign and house it leads you to what is unfamiliar and new. It's both the road and the Quest itself. It takes the old personal story and says: "why not this, instead of this?" The North Node holds the homeopathic medicine that leads you away from the distractions and habits that keep you from creating the new story of your life and from being your authentic Self.

Authentic Self? So how do you know when you are truly being you? What story about yourself are you buying into now? You may be getting married, divorced, or going off on a new adventure to Barcelona or Peru, but what "distractions" will you carry with you that will keep you from being open to the new experience? Yes, it's the baggage of the South Node distractions that we all bring with us, and we need to "repack our bags" if we are going to truly open up to something new in life.

The "Quest for the Authentic Self" is a great idea in theory and rings true for spiritual seekers whether we are existentialists, astrologers, or Buddhists. In this quest we're looking at maps in the form of books and charts, and we are looking to unleash the silenced voices in the psyche. We're also listening to others, and the truths they speak. We're questing for new questions, new answers, and risking the journey; we're willing to be brave.

The Buddhists remind us that we suffer because we're attached to specific outcomes and permanence. The Existentialists remind us of the necessity to use our freedom and free will in creating an authentic Self, and the astrologers remind us that we're not alone—that we fit into a larger meaningful pattern in the Cosmos, and that there is much that is unconscious within us.

I believe that as we discover the many planetary "voices" that live within each of us, we find that these archetypal symbols—these planets and Nodes —point the way to a larger and more authentic life than we've ever known. And as for me, I'm in a new process of "re-packing my bags" with a North Node Directional Map—which means I'm looking at how I distract myself from a more authentic relationship with myself, with others, and with my work. I'm going to delve deeper into my Taurus North Node to find what resources and values are truly waiting to be lived. Once I release myself from all the distracting stories I tell myself about myself —all those old South Node Scorpion-ic stories of "how it all was and how it still is"....well, then I'll have time and space in my life to open up to a deeper more authentic life. It all takes time and compassion, but I'm ready to bring on the new! What about you?

Where is my South Node?

June 7, 1913-Dec. 3, 1914: Virgo

Dec. 4, 1914-May 31, 1916: Leo

June 1, 1916-Feb. 13, 1918: Cancer

Feb. 14, 1918-Aug. 15, 1919: Gemini

Aug. 16, 1919-Feb. 7, 1921: Taurus

Feb. 8, 1921-Aug. 23, 1922: Aries

Aug. 24, 1922-Apr.23, 1924: Pisces

April 24, 1924-Oct. 26,1925: Aquarius

Oct. 27, 1925-Apr.16,1927: Capricorn

Apr.17,1927-Dec.28,1928: Sagittarius

Dec.29,1928-July 7,1930: Scorpio

July 8,1930-Dec.28,1931: Libra

Dec.29,1931-June 24, 1933: Virgo

June 25, 1933-Mar.8,1935: Leo

Mar 9, 1935-Sept. 14, 1936: Cancer

Sept. 15, 1936-Mar. 3, 1938: Gemini

Mar. 4, 1938-Sept. 12, 1939: Taurus

Sept. 13, 1939-May 24, 1941: Aries

May 25, 1941-Nov. 21,1942: Pisces

Nov. 22, 1942-May 11, 1944: Aquarius

May 12, 1944-Dec. 13, 1945: Capricorn

Dec. 14,1945-Aug. 2, 1947: Sagittarius

Aug. 3, 1947-Jan. 26,1949: Scorpio

Jan. 27,1949-Jul 26,1950: Libra

Jul 27, 1950-Mar.28,1952: Virgo

Mar.29, 1952-Oct. 9, 1953:Leo

Oct.10,1953-Apr.2, 1955: Cancer

Apr 3,1955-Oct.4,1956: Gemini

Oct.5,1956-June 16,1958: Taurus

Jun. 17,1958-Dec.15,1959: Aries

Dec.16,1959-Jun 10,1961: Pisces

June 11,1961-Dec.23,1962: Aquarius

Dec.24,1962-Aug.25,1964: Capricorn

Aug.26,1964-Feb.19,1966: Sagittarius

Feb.20,1966-Aug.19,1967: Scorpio

Aug.20,1967-Apr.19,1969: Libra

Apr.20,1969-Nov.2,1970: Virgo

Nov.3,1970-Apr.27,1972: Leo

Apr.28,1972-Oct.27,1973: Cancer

Oct.28,1973-Jul 10,1975: Gemini

Jul 11, 1975-Jan. 7, 1977: Taurus

Jan. 8, 1977-Jul 5,1978: Aries

Jul 6 1978-Jan.12,1980: Pisces

Jan.13,1980-Sept.24,1981: Aquarius

Sept.25,1981-Mar.16,1983: Capricorn

Mar.17.1983-Sept.11,1984: Sagittarius

Sept.12,1984-Apr.6,1986: Scorpio

Apr.7,1986-Dec.2,1987: Libra

Dec.3,1987-May 22, 1989: Virgo

May 23, 1989-Nov.18,1990: Leo

Nov.19,1990-Aug. 1,1992: Cancer

Aug.2,1992-Feb.1,1994: Gemini

Feb.2,1994-Jul 31, 1995: Taurus

Aug.1,1995-Jan.25,1997: Aries

Jan.26,1997-Oct.20,1998: Pisces

Oct. 21, 1998-Apr.9,2000: Aquarius

Apr.10,2000-Oct.12,2001: Capricorn

Oct.13,2001-Apr.13,2003: Sagittarius

Apr.14,2003-Dec.25,2004: Scorpio

Dec.26,2004-Jun 21, 2006: Libra

Jun 22,2006-Dec.18, 2007: Virgo

Dec. 19, 2007-Aug 22 2009: Leo

(For more recent dates google your South Node sign for your birthday and year)

ABOUT THE AUTHOR

Elizabeth Spring, M.A., has a degree in counseling astrology with an emphasis in the work of Carl Jung. She began her astrological studies with Isabel Hickey in Boston in 1969, and has continued studying (and certification) with astrologers Steven Forrest, Alice Howell, and Liz Greene. She has done post-graduate work at Pacifica Institute in California, Salve Regina University, and Krotona Institute of Theosophy. She teaches periodically at the Boston Jung Institute and has lectured at Brown University, RISD, and yoga centers around New England. Elizabeth has been a psychotherapist and practicing astrologer since 1992. This is her sixth book. All her books are available on amazon.com and can be bought as a paperback, e-book, or audible book.

For more information check out her website: NorthNodeAstrology.com, or the Podcast at "North Node Astrology" on Apple Podcasts, or blog: SouthNodeAstrology.blogspot.com, or email her at elizabethspring@aol.com

Made in the USA
Las Vegas, NV
15 June 2024